*Larry H_____*

W9-CVY-407

# GOD LISTENS

## to the crying heart
## in the secret place

by

*Samuel*

*Chadwick*

*Published by*
**GOOD NEWS PUBLISHERS**
Westchester, Illinois 60153
*in cooperation with*
**THE GREAT COMMISSION PRAYER LEAGUE**

*Copyright* © 1973
**GOOD NEWS PUBLISHERS**
Westchester, Illinois 60153

*in cooperation with*
**THE GREAT COMMISSION PRAYER LEAGUE**

*All rights reserved*
*printed in the United States of America*

This edition of *God Listens* has been especially printed for distribution by Radio Bible Class, Grand Rapids, Michigan 49501.

# Contents

## Foreword

The chapters of this book were written for <u>Joyful News</u> Mission which was born of the prayers of Thomas and Mary Champness as they prayed one morning between the hours of four and five. It is a witness to the teaching of this book concerning the power of prayer. The articles were not written for critics nor for scholars, but for plain people who are deeply religious and sincerely simple in their trust. Hundreds of readers wrote asking that the articles should be put into a book. If they had been written for a book they might have lost the artlessness of a simple purpose. They are sent forth in the form in which it pleased God to bless them.

# I. The Sign of Prayer

All religions pray. God and prayer are inseparable. Belief in God and belief in prayer are elemental and intuitive. The ideas may be crude and cruel in primitive and pagan peoples, but they belong to the universal intuitions of the human race. The teaching of the Old Testament is full of the subject of prayer. Everywhere there are commands and inducements to pray, and the great stories of deliverance and victory, experience and vision, are all examples of prevailing prayer. All the crises in the life of our Lord were linked with special seasons of prayer, and His teaching set forth wonderful assurances to those who pray. He laid down the laws of prayer, though He never sought to explain its mystery. Prayer was not a problem to Him. The two parables He spoke about prayer are not very acceptable to those who pray. There is something alien to the spirit of prayer in likening God to a heartless judge or a churlish friend. God is neither. The parables were not spoken as representative of God, but to illustrate the reward of importunity.

The basis of prayer is sonship. Prayer is possible and reasonable because it is filial. It is natural for a child to ask of its father, and it is reasonable for the father to listen to the request of his child. "If ye, then, being evil, know how to give good gifts unto your children, how much more shall your Father which is in Heaven give good things to them that ask Him" Matt. 7:7-11; Thess. 11:9-13.

There are many problems about prayer, but they lie outside the fact and experience of prayer, and apart from praying there is no solution of them. Prayer is a fact of experience, and through all the ages the testimony of those who prayed has been that God hears and answers the prayers of His children.

## What God Thinks about Prayer

The thoughts of God are not as man's thoughts, neither are His ways as man's ways. "As the heavens are higher than the earth, so are God's ways higher than man's ways, and His thoughts than man's thoughts" Isa. 55:8, 9. God has made known His thoughts and His ways, in the revelation of His Word and in the Person of His Son. The medium of the revelation is experience, and the occasion is in the events of life in individuals and in history. God has never put His thoughts into a thesis of philosophy or metaphysics. He has interpreted in life and set forth His ways in precepts, principles, and example. His mind concerning prayer is seen in every command to pray, in every law of prayer, in every promise concerning prayer, and in every example of answered prayer. Each is part of the whole, but has its final and complete expression.

In the conversion of Saul of Tarsus there is a unique revelation of the mind of God concerning prayer. There are three persons in that incident of prayer. There is the man who prayed, the God who heard, and the man through whom the answer came. God is central. It is to Him prayer is made, through Him prayer is interpreted, and by Him prayer is answered.

God speaks of prayer in terms of wonder: "Behold, he prayeth" Acts 9:11. The language is that of humanity, but it is the only speech man knows, and however inadequate it may be, it stands for corresponding reality in God. Can there be in Him elements of surprise and amazement? Can it be that there are things that to God are wonderful? To Him there is nothing more gloriously wonderful than prayer. It would seem as if the biggest thing in God's universe is a man who prays. The only thing more amazing is that man, knowing this, should not pray. Behold! In that word there is rapture, exultation. In the estimate of God prayer is more glorious than all the mysteries of the earth, more mighty than all the forces of creation.

God interprets prayer as a sign of all that happened to Saul of Tarsus on the Damascus road. The event is variously expressed. To the Churches of Judaea it was a conversion that turned their arch persecutor into a preacher. Apostle Paul states in Galatians, "Afterwards I came into the regions of Syria and Cilicia; and was unknown by face unto the Churches of Judaea which were in Christ; But they had heard only, that he which persecuted us in times past now preacheth the faith which once he destroyed. And they glorified God in me," 1:21-24. That conversion was the result of an experience in which Paul says it pleased God to reveal His Son in him. That is what the Damascus road experience meant to him. When God speaks of it He sums it all up in the words, "Behold, he prayeth."

Prayer is the symbol and proof and gauge of grace. All that happens in the converting work of grace whereby we receive the adoption of sons is that, being sons, we begin to pray. Saul of Tarsus had been a praying man all his life, but it was not until he came into God's family that he began to pray as God interprets prayer. The children's hymn is equally applicable to grown-up people:

> *"I often say my prayers,*
> *But do I ever pray?"*

Prayer is the privilege of sons, and the test of sonship. It would seem as if God divides all men into the simple classification of those who pray and those who do not. It is a very simple test, but it is decisive, and divisive.

### The Way God Answers Prayer

God answers joyously. There is a ring of exultation in the words He speaks to Ananias, like the joyous ring of our Lord's Parable of the Lost Sheep, the Lost Coin, and the Lost Son. Rejoice with Me! "Behold, he prayeth!" There is joy in the heart of God the Father when His lost children begin to pray. He answers like the God He is. Ananias may parley with God, but God never parleys with man. The answering hand of God waits for the lifted hand of man, and the heart that answers always transcends the heart that cries.

The answer to Saul of Tarsus was twofold: He gave a vision and sent a messenger—a vision, and a man, each corresponding to the other. This is God's way: first assurance, and then confirmation. This is the prayer of faith that never fails. God's servants are partners with Him in the ministry of prayer. This is the mystery of spiritual co-operation. The Lord goes before the man He sends. Saul was prepared and waiting for the man he had already seen in a vision of God. Ananias found Saul prepared and waiting.

God gave to Ananias the sign of prayer as the

proof of grace. It was His own sign, and it is the
sign He still gives. Is there any proof that a man is a
man of God like the fact that he is a man of
prayer? Of Elijah it is said that he "prayed in his
prayer" James 5:17, A.V. margin. Of some men it
is said that they live in an atmosphere of devotion;
but it is one thing to live in an atmosphere of
prayer, and another to "pray in our praying."
Finney went to a weekly prayer-meeting, where
they prayed much and got no answers. Muller
prayed and answers came, and that is why all men
believed him to be a man of God.

When I was a very small boy, I was sent on an
errand to the house of a neighbor about nine
o'clock in the morning. I knocked and stepped in-
side. On the hearth, kneeling at a chair on which
was an open Bible, was Mrs. Davenport, praying.
She was unaware of my presence. I stood in silent
awe for a moment, and then quietly stepped out
and closed the door. It is more than sixty years
since that morning, but from then till now I have
known that Mrs. Davenport was a saint of God,
because she prayed. It is God's infallible sign, and
it is the only sign that even the world accepts as an
infallible proof.

Prayer made all the difference to Saul of Tarsus,
and it always makes all the difference. It brings a
new assurance of God, a new confirmation of faith,
a new fellowship of the people of God, a new experience of healing, a new vocation, a new inheritance, a new power. Prayer changes things. Prayer
makes all things possible, for it links the praying
soul to the omnipotence of God. Do we pray? Do
we pray in our praying? Does God put His seal on
our prayer?

Lord, teach us to pray!

Prayer is the contrite sinner's voice
Returning from his ways,
While angels in their songs rejoice,
And cry, Behold he prays.

Prayer is the Christian's vital breath,
The Christian's native air,
His watchword at the gates of death,
He enters heaven with prayer.

## 2. Learning to Pray

Can prayer be learned? Is it not of the very soul
of prayer that it should be in the freedom of the
Spirit? John the Baptist gave his disciples a form of
prayer, and the disciples of Jesus asked to be
taught to pray. There were not many things they
asked Him to do for them, and when they did they
were usually wrong. Would He have given them a
form of prayer if they had not asked Him? Why
did they ask? His own praying awoke within them
a desire to be able to pray, and when they wanted
to pray they found they did not know how. They
felt the need of some ordered form by which they
could speak out of their heart to God. They
quoted John. There are still disciples who quote
John the Baptist to Jesus.

Forms are easier than a creative spirit. Prayers
counted on a Rosary are easier than the prayers of
a soul poured out in unrestrained speech to God.
The Prayer Book helps the inarticulate to expres-

sion. Such praying may be perfectly sincere, and
the devout may find in provided prayers a real help
to devotion. But it is not other people's prayers
that make the man of prayer. True prayer, the
prayer that prevails, is personal, intimate, and original.

Hannah protested that she had poured out her
soul to God. That is prayer, and yet it is not the
whole of prayer. Receptivity is as real a part of
prayer as expression. Saul of Tarsus never really
prayed till he met the Risen Lord on the Damascus
road. From the heavenward side the whole change
that had been wrought was summed up in the
words, "Behold, he prayeth."

The secret of Elijah's power in prayer was that
he "prayed in his prayer." That is the translation
given in the margin of the Authorized Version. He
"prayed earnestly" is given in the text, and "fervently" in the Revised Version, with the note in
the margin that the Greek literally is, "with
prayer." He prayed with prayer; he prayed in his
prayer. He did not say prayers; he prayed in praying. His whole personality was in his supplication.
He really wanted what he asked, and fervently
meant what he said. Can that kind of prayer be
taught?

It is the prayer that prevails. Formal routine
reading of others' words are neither acceptable to
God nor profitable to man. They are vain repetitions. There is much praying that avails nothing, so
far as we can judge. Prayers are measured neither
by time nor by number, but by intensity. There are
prayers that are impassioned and there is no answer, and there are things for which we know we
ought to pray in an agony of prayer, and there is
no power to pray. We do not know how to pray.

# Prayer Learned by Praying

There is no way to learn but by praying. No reasoned philosophy of prayer ever taught a soul to pray. The subject is beset with problems, but there are no problems to the one who prays. They are all met in the fact of answered prayer and the joy of fellowship with God. We know not what we should pray for as we ought, and if prayer waits for understanding it will never begin. We live by faith. We walk by faith. Thomas A. Edison: "We don't know the millionth part of one per cent about anything. We don't know what water is. We don't know what light is. We don't know what gravitation is. We don't know what enables us to keep on our feet when we stand up. We don't know what electricity is. We don't know what heat is. We don't know anything about magnetism. We have a lot of hypotheses about these things, but that is all. But we do not let our ignorance about all these things deprive us of their use." We discover by using. We learn by practice. Though a man should have all knowledge about prayer, and though he understand all mysteries about prayer, unless he prays he will never learn to pray.

Those who became mighty in prayer, learned to pray. There was a period in their lives when they were as others in the matter of prayer. In every instance there was a crisis of grace, but it was in the discipline of grace that they discovered the secret of power. They were known as men of God, because they were men of prayer. Some of them like Jacob and Simon and Saul were renamed, "Praying John," "Praying Bramwell," and "Praying Hyde." Praying men saved England by prayer. They shook the Gates of Hell by prayer. They

opened the windows of Heaven by prayer. They
learned to pray by being much in prayer. They did not talk about prayer; they prayed. They did not argue about prayer; they prayed.

## Trained in Prayer

Prayer touches infinite extremes. It is so simple that a little child can pray, and it is so profound that none but a child-heart can pray. Montgomery's hymn has immortalized its profound simplicity:

*Prayer is the soul's sincere desire,*
  *Uttered or unexpressed,*
*The motion of a hidden fire*
  *That trembles in the breast.*

*Prayer is the simplest form of speech*
  *That infant lips can try;*
*Prayer the sublimest strains that reach*
  *The Majesty on High.*

That is gloriously true. A cry brings God. A cry is mightier than the polished phrase. The Pharisee prayed within himself. His prayers revolved on ruts of vanity in his mind and heart. The publican cried and was heard. It is not of emergency exits of the soul we are thinking, but the sustained habit and experience of the man of prayer. Such prayer comes by training, and there is no discipline so exacting. Coleridge says of such praying that it is the very highest energy of which the human heart is capable, and it calls for the total concentration of all the faculties. The great mass of worldly men and learned men he pronounced incapable of prayer. To pray as God would have us pray is the greatest achievement on earth.

Such a life of prayer costs. It takes time. Hurried

**14** prayers and muttered litanies can never produce souls mighty in prayer. Learners give hours regularly every day that they may become proficient in art and mechanism. Our Lord rose before daybreak that He might pray, and not infrequently He spent all night in prayer. All praying saints have spent hours every day in prayer.

In these days there is no time to pray; but without taking time, we shall never learn to pray. It ought to be possible to give God one hour out of twenty-four all to Himself. Let us make a start in the discipline of training in prayer by setting apart a fixed time every day for the exercise of prayer. We must seriously set our hearts to learn how to pray. A great saint once said, "Believe me, to pray with all your heart and strength, with the reason and the will, to believe vividly that God will listen to your voice through Christ, and verily do the thing He pleaseth thereupon—this is the last, the greatest achievement of the Christian's warfare upon earth."

Teach us to pray, O Lord, we beseech Thee.

> *The praying Spirit breathe,*
> *The watching power impart,*
> *From all entanglements beneath,*
> *Call off my anxious heart.*

> *My feeble mind sustain,*
> *By worldly thoughts oppressed,*
> *Appear, and bid me turn again*
> *To my eternal rest.*

When you feel the strain of discipline remember these words:

> *. . . Thou art oft most present, Lord,*
> *In weak, distracted prayer;*
> *A sinner out of heart with self,*
> *Most often finds Thee there.*

*For prayer that humbles sets the soul*
*From all delusions free,*
*And teaches it how utterly*
*Dear Lord, it hangs on Thee.*

## 3. Praying in Secret

If prayer is the greatest achievement on earth, we may be sure it calls for a discipline that corresponds to its power. The School of Prayer has its conditions and demands. It is a forbidden place to all but those of set purpose and resolute heart. Strong men often break down under the strain of study. Concentration is a heavier task than handling a hammer or guiding a plough. The discipline curbs freedom, and drills the mind to attention. Understanding is more taxing than doing, and meditation is a severer tax than service. The reason so many people do not pray is because of its cost. The cost is not so much in the sweat of agonizing supplication, as in the daily fidelity to the life of prayer. It is the test of devotion. Nothing in the life of faith is so difficult to maintain.

There are those who resent the association of discipline and intensity with prayer. They do not pray like that, and certainly they would not like their children to entreat and plead for anything they want with "strong crying and tears." That is quite likely, but then no one suspects them of praying like that, and the analogy of their children may not be the whole truth. Nothing can be farther from the truth than a false analogy. The School of Prayer is for those who really want to learn to pray.

## The Secret Place

Those who come to learn are disciples. They put themselves under the yoke of Him from Whom they seek to learn, and the first condition of learning is a teachable spirit. Our Lord has the authority to teach, and He is the Example as well as Instructor. There is no appeal beyond Him. Having asked Him to teach us how to pray, we surrender mind and heart to His teaching and yield all to the discipline of loyal and believing obedience.

One of the first things He commands is that there be a place of prayer. It is quite true that the whole earth is the Lord's, and that there is no place where prayer cannot be heard. Wherever there is a praying heart, the soul finds the sanctuary of God. No one would suggest that Jesus did not appreciate the sacredness of the earth, which He said was the footstool of God, but it was His habit to withdraw into a solitary place to pray. He needed the fenced spaces of silence. To His disciples He said:

"And when ye pray, ye shall not be as the hypocrites: for they love to stand and pray in the synagogues and in the corners of the streets that they may be seen of men. Verily I say unto you, they have received their reward. But thou, when thou prayest, enter into thine inner chamber, and having shut thy door, pray to thy Father which is in secret, and thy Father which seeth in secret shall recompense thee" Matt. 6:5, 6.

Why does He insist on this inner chamber? One

reason is that the first quality God requires in
prayer is reality. Hypocrites never pray in secret.
Prayers that are a pretence require an audience.
They are intended to be heard of men, and they
have their reward in skill of phrasing, a show of
earnestness, and a reputation for piety. These do
not count with God. They cannot live in His presence. Prayer is between the soul and God alone.

## The Silent Spaces of the Soul

The soul needs its silent spaces. It is in them we
learn to pray. There shut in with God, our Lord
bids us pray to our Father who is in secret, and
sees in secret. There is no test like solitude. Fear
takes possession of most minds in the stillness of
the solitary place. The heart shrinks from being
alone with God. Who shall abide in His presence?
Who can dwell with God Who is shadowless light?
Hearts must be pure and hands clean that dare shut
the door and be alone with God. It would revolu-
tionize the lives of most men if they were shut in
with God in some secret place for half an hour a
day.

For such praying all the faculties of the soul
need to be alert. When our Lord took Peter and
James and John with Him to the secret place of
prayer, they were sleepy. It was the same in the
Mount of Glory and the Garden of Agony, and it
was not until they were fully awake that they saw
the glory or realized the anguish. Mooning is not
meditation, and drowsy repose is not praying. The
secret place of prayer calls for every faculty of
mind and heart.

*"Bless the Lord, O my soul;*
*And all that is within me*
*Bless His Holy Name."*

**18** There is a vital difference between private and corporate prayer. Each kind of prayer brings blessing after its kind, but there is a difference. Corporate prayer is less exacting. There is a sense of fellowship that gives courage and inspires expression. Guided prayer is companionable, but it has a tendency to do its thinking by proxy. In private prayer the soul stands naked and alone in the presence of God. Thought is personal, prayer is original, motive is challenged. Private prayer disciplines personality. Who can measure the influence of an hour a day spent alone with God?

### The Hill of the Lord

The way into the Holy Presence is not a thoroughfare. The quiet room into which a man goes is his own, but it is the Presence of God that makes it a Holy Place. To a secular mind there would be no Presence. It is the seeking soul that finds. There are some people to whom no audience is given. There are souls who cannot pray. James says of some men that they need not think they can receive anything of the Lord. Even before Christ taught men to pray, the Psalmist declared, "If I regard iniquity in my heart, the Lord will not hear" Ps. 66:18. The Judgment Seat of God is in the inner chamber; but the Throne of Grace is there also, or none would ever dare to enter. Forgotten and hidden things stand naked and open before Him with Whom we have to do. All who desire to enter the Holy Presence and live, must have a sincere desire for God and a conscience set on dwelling in the light.

Again, when Jesus stated the law of faith in relation to prayer, He said: "Therefore I say unto you, all things whatsoever ye pray and ask for, believe that ye have received them, and ye shall have them.

And whensoever ye pray, forgive, if ye have aught against any one; that your Father also which is in heaven may forgive you your trespasses, but if ye do not forgive, neither will your Father which is in heaven forgive your trespasses" Mark 11:24-26.

Our Lord emphasized the forgiving spirit. The one thing above all others that bolts and bars the way into the Presence Chamber of Prayer is unwillingness to forgive from the heart. No gift can be accepted of God until reconciliation has been made. "If therefore thou art offering thy gift at the altar, and there rememberest that thy brother hath aught against thee, leave there thy gift before the altar, and go thy way, first be reconciled to thy brother, and then come and offer thy gift" Matt. 5:23, 24.

Why did He emphasize forgiveness? Was it not for the same reason that the Law and Prophets placed emphasis on righteousness? All who would come to the Holy One must be holy, and whoever will come to the God of Mercy must be merciful. The petitioner for grace must believe in grace.

### "Thine Inner Chamber"

Let no soul be discouraged from starting. Schools are graded to the capacity of the learners. The great souls who became mighty in prayer, and rejoiced to spend three and four hours a day alone with God, were once beginners. They went from strength to strength. For our comfort let us remember that it is into our own inner chamber we enter, and the God Who is there is our Father.

Many years ago a sweet little girl stole into my bedroom in the house where I was staying. She prattled blithely about the wonders of her child world, but when I asked if her father was up, she looked radiantly and reverently into my eyes and said, "Oh, my daddy always talks with God in the drawing room before breakfast."

Happy father! Happy child! Happy God!

# 4. The Inner Room and the Closed Door

"But thou, when thou prayest, enter into thine inner chamber, and having shut thy door, pray to thy Father which is in secret, and thy Father which seeth in secret shall recompense thee" Matt. 6:5, 6.

There are two difficulties awaiting us at the threshold of his command. One is that many have no inner chamber. There is no place in their lives for privacy. They have no room that is not shared, and if they could find room they have no leisure. The closed door may neither shut out nor shut in. The radio made us familiar with the fact that neither bolted doors nor shuttered windows can secure privacy. Thought is more subtle than sound, and Satan is more cunning than the radio expert. The saints who have been practiced in private prayer bear witness to the adversaries that keep watch at the door of the soul's inner chamber.

### Where Shall We Find the Secret Place?

My aim is not to instruct, but to suggest. Manuals of devotion have usually been to me depressing rather than helpful. They are either too mechanical or too exacting. They discourage rather than inspire. I am writing frankly, and in the first person. All my life I have wanted to learn to pray. In my zeal I have experimented and explored in likely and unlikely ways and schools of prayer, and without pride I want in humility to tell you what I have learned. I speak for myself. I judge no man's method, criticize no man's counsel, challenge no man's experience. I speak with simplicity, and you must judge what I say.

Let us begin with the difficulty of privacy. Many of Christ's disciples have no room to which they can retire for private prayer. They live with other people, sleep with other people, work with other people. They cannot escape from people. Is not this a reason why the door of the House of God should never be closed?

One Monday morning a penitent sinner stopped me in the main street of the town where I had preached on the Sunday. There were three churches near at hand, but they were locked, and we had to go to the parish church to find a place where there was privacy for prayer. The door of a church should always be open. Even that does not meet the need of the soul. The secret place of prayer should be part of daily life, a part of the daily dwelling-place.

Some place must be found that can be a trysting-place with God. A hungry heart will find a way. Perhaps in the open air or in some secluded corner, a place may be found. If this is impossible, the soul must make an open space into which it can withdraw, even in the presence of others, and be alone with God. The place of His Glory is in the solitudes, where He hides us in the cleft of the rock, and talks with us face to face as one talks with a friend.

## How can We Secure the Closed Door?

How is it possible to keep the world from coming in and the mind from straying out? Concentration on any subject is a severe strain on the mind, and no where is it so difficult as in private prayer. An enemy is there to raise bogies, excite conscience, jog memory, and direct invaders of the sacred hour. Some simple device will usually secure the secret place from intrusion. General Gordon pinned a white handkerchief at the opening of his tent. I hang a card outside the door when I wish to be alone. This is simple enough, but though it may keep people out, it is useless against the distractions of the mind, and a body may just as well be roaming at large as be shut in with a wandering mind. How can distractions be shut out?

Attention is an act of the will. Concentration is sustained attention upon a specific object. The will can be disciplined and the power of concentration developed. An educated mind is trained to attention and concentration. By patience the soul is won, and by discipline the mind is trained. God is in secret. Let the first act be to affirm the fact of the Holy Presence. Call every faculty of mind and body to remembrance, recognition, and realization of the God that is in secret and sees in secret. Hold the mind to this fact. Tolerate no distraction, allow no diversion, indulge no dissipation. Prayer in the secret place demands every faculty at its best.

Our Lord gave His disciples a form and order of prayer, and it does not begin with either song or supplication, but with the contemplation of God:

Our Father,

All the great prayers of the Bible begin this way. I find it helpful to begin this way too. I think in adoring love and wonder of His character and attributes, of His majesty and might, of His grace and glory. Musing kindles the fire, and the flame becomes "a wall of fire round about," which keeps beasts and intruders at a safe distance. I often find that prayer in the secret place begins with the Doxology, and abounds in glory and thanksgiving. It is there the Transfigured Lord is seen.

### The Word of God in the Holy Presence

I never take any book but the Bible into the secret place. It is my prayer book. I seek no external aids to devotion, such as the Cross or Crucifix. I have no altar but the one within the veil. Other minds have other ways. Most people have some devotional classic, but I do not take even my hymn-book. I will write more fully on the devotional use of the Bible, and at present I will content myself with saying that I feed upon it by searching its truth, appropriating its affirmations, and turning its Psalms and prayers into personal thanksgiving and supplication. Questions of criticism, textual or otherwise, do not enter into my mind in the secret place, any more than questions of chemical analysis trouble me when I eat my dinner. The Word is more to me than my necessary food. It thrills and moves me with tremendous power.

The Word of God instructs us how to pray. Normally, to kneel is reverent and helpful. One of my friends tells me that he sits, and close by him he places a vacant chair. The habit should be to kneel, but conditions of health and soul will dictate their own posture. It is fitting that we should "kneel before the Lord our Maker." Ps. 95:6. Prayer is more than asking, but even our asking should be instructed by the Holy Spirit. I find it good to rehearse and review my daily life in the Holy Presence. It is there I make my plans. God keeps the pattern of earthly things in the Holy Mount. Thomas Champness talked with God about his work and his evangelists every morning from five to six. God guides with His eye, and eyes speak best in the place of secret communion. It is there we are assured of His will and are made to understand His way.

It is the place of Intercession. That is the place where we can talk freely with God about other people. The family, the Church, the business, the friendships, the state, the world, are all subjects of earnest and believing private prayer. Class leaders should go over the classbook name by name; the Sunday School superintendent over the teachers' roll, and the teacher over the class register in the same way, name by name. Keep a prayer list of subjects for intercession, and always have a list of people for whom you pray. It is not necessary to tell anyone else what you tell God. The Father is in secret, He sees in secret, He hears in secret; leave it to Him to make it known.

The God in secret is our Father. Prayer is filial; we pray as sons and daughters in the Father's House. He knows our need better than we can tell Him, and He is able to do exceeding abundantly above all we can ask or think; therefore ask in confidence, nothing doubting. It is in the secret place we learn that silence is the best speech and listening is the best part of praying. Those who speak are heard, and those who listen hear. Of

Jesus it is said: "And in the morning, a great while
before day, He rose up and went out, and departed
into a solitary place, and there prayed" Mark 1:35.

# 5. The Word of God and Prayer

The Word of God quickens the soul and instructs it in prayer. The Psalmist speaks for all who
pray when he confesses to seasons when the soul
cannot find its wings: "My soul cleaveth unto the
dust; quicken Thou me according to Thy Word"
Ps. 119:25. It is always to the Word of God he
turns for quickening and instruction. Paul links together the Word of God and prayer. "And take . . .
the sword of the Spirit which is the Word of God;
praying always with all prayer and supplication,
and watching thereunto with all perseverance and
supplication for all saints; and for me" Eph. 6:18.
Watching where and whereunto? Watching with all
perseverance! That is surely with diligence and
patience, alertness and reverence. We must search
the Word, that we may know how to pray. "God is
a Spirit; and they that worship Him must worship
Him in spirit and in truth" John 4:24.

### Aids to Devotion

I do not judge any man in the method of devotion.
I speak only for myself. The practice of private
prayer is so difficult to maintain, that I don't be-
grudge help to those who find aid in things that to
me are a hindrance. Some find help in symbols and
pictures, and most of those who seek to cultivate

the prayer life of the soul keep some book of devotion at hand. Thomas a Kempis, Lancelot Andrewes, William Law, Andrew Murray, and the hymnology of all the churches have been blessed to tens of thousands who have sought to know how to pray. It may be a confession of shame, but I do not want any of them in the "inner chamber." I can appreciate them, more or less, elsewhere, but not here.

There are two perils to be avoided: one is emotional unreality; and the other is intellectual preoccupation. An earnest believer whose religious enthusiasm found expression in service for the Church and humanity was convicted of prayerlessness. He earnestly resolved to spend half an hour every day in private prayer. At the end of a month he gave it up because he could not endure the sense of unreality. He could not talk or meditate half an hour every day when there was no one there! There was not only no sense of a Presence, but there was a very real consciousness of an absence. There can be no experience of heart speech and soul fellowship without a consciousness of a Presence. The soul cannot keep up an emotional make-believe day after day. The mind cannot live in a vacuum. The Father is in secret, but it is the glory of His Presence that makes the sanctuary. There must be truth as well as spirit in all worship, and nowhere is the combination more necessary than in the secret place of prayer.

Altar fires are kindled and quickened by truth, but the truth must get to the Altar. Devotional studies do not necessarily lead to devotion. There may be a preoccupation with truth that becomes an obsession. The study of experimental truth may never become experience, and the experience of

others may become a snare. Even the Bible may
become a hindrance. Light can blind. Our Lord reproached the religious teachers of His day because their misuse of the Scriptures blinded their minds. Stepping-stones may become slipping-stones, and even a cornerstone may be a stumbling block. In all questions of the soul each must find help where he can.

## The Devotional Use of the Bible

Do we still have a Bible we can take into the Holy Place? The most disastrous result of paganizing the Bible is that it has so largely fallen into disuse as a book of devotion. An honest man cannot pray through a discredited book. Truth is as essential to man as to God. Some modernist teachers and preachers have what the learned call a "complex." The unlearned call it a "bee in the bonnet." They never miss a chance to drag in a jibe at what they call the traditional view of the Bible, and yet they insist that nothing has been lost in the change. The Scriptures are still "the living and sovereign Word of God." They admit that "Jesus took the Bible at its face value," and that in it He found His Gospel, on it He fed His soul, and in all the great crises of His life relied upon its truth. The disciple may be content to be as his Lord.

There are methods of Bible study that do not belong to the inner sanctuary of prayer. Historical sources, literary criticism, higher criticism, and lower criticism belong to the forum and the study. They are concerned with the external conditions and progressive development of revealed truth. In the Holy Place the Scriptures are received as "the living, sovereign Word of God." "Holy men of God spake as they were moved by the Holy Ghost" 2

Peter 1:21. Questions of date, authorship, and the like are left outside, not because ignorance is more helpful to prayer than intelligence, but because they are irrelevant.

In all Scripture there is a local and immediate message of truth, but there is also a revelation that is timeless and universal. Local knowledge is essential to complete understanding, but the soul in prayer comes to the Word that it may find God, and to the soul at prayer it is the infallible, sovereign, saving Word of God. Therefore we may still take the Scriptures into the inner chamber. Even the critics are anxious to assure us that the things for which they contend are not among the things that really matter, and, after all, their "assured results" are nothing more than "agreed hypotheses."

I do not want to harp unduly on the subject of Biblical criticism, but I think it may help you if I tell you how I regard the Scriptures. It always seems to me that there is a very real analogy between the Word of the Lord and the law of the land. The judge and jury accept the law, and it is their business, not to criticize or amend, but to interpret and administer. They have no concern with the politics and politicians by whom the law came. It is very interesting to study the historical situation. it was intended to meet, to trace the agitation of the reformers, to know who framed the Bill, and who was responsible for amending clauses, but that is the business of historians, experts, and antiquarians. Even a lawyer may be ignorant of them. His business is to know the law. The business of a judge is to interpret the law. The business of the jury is to submit their verdict to the authority of the law.

So it is with the Word of God. There may be

two Isaiahs or twenty, two contributors to the Pentateuch or two hundred, Mark's Gospel may have begun with "Q" or any other letter of the alphabet. The Word has passed beyond personal and historical limitations, and because of the Inspiration that gave them, the Scriptures are the Word of the Lord that abideth for ever. We take the Bible into the inner sanctuary, not that we may know what is its literary history, but that we may hear what the Lord our God will say to us.

### The Praying Method in the Word

Paul said, "I will pray with the understanding also" I Cor. 14:15. The Word of God gives understanding to prayer. The Bible is not an easy Book to the uninitiated, and that is why so many fall back on ordered and simple books of devotion, but it is the Book of Common Prayer to be understood by the common people.

The first question is where to begin. Each will find his own starting point. I began with the Psalms. The next thing to decide is the most suitable time of the day. When I began I was called at five o'clock in the morning, and had to be at work at six, so I read my morning portion the night before. I read through the appointed portion in a prayer spirit again and again, then went over it clause by clause on my knees, turning its statements into prayer and thanksgiving. Then I wrote out the verse or phrase that spoke to me, read it over next morning as I dressed, committed the day briefly to God, and put the text in my waistcoat pocket. Before I found this method I used to try to work myself into a praying mood, but I lacked resourcefulness, and praying became "prayers" again, and listening a void. Prayer has been an experience of thrilling wonder, creative meditation, and real fellowship since it has been instructed, quickened, and inspired by the Word of God.

In addition to this simple method, I find great help in the use of the marginal references, especially those of the Revised Version. The method taught by the Holy Spirit is to compare Scripture with Scripture, and spiritual things with spiritual. The Spirit that inspired the Scriptures is given to us for interpretation. The Holy Spirit and the Holy Word are never at variance. Revelation is progressive, and every part has its relative truth. To watch the unfolding of the Word deeply stirs my soul. New discoveries excite the mind and kindle the fires of worship and praise. Is this prayer? It assuredly is, so long as it is kept to its devotional purpose, and not followed with any other object. I once tried taking Scriptures I was studying for examination as my devotional portion, but it left the hour barren and unprofitable. God wants the whole presence of the spirit, as surely as man wants the sense of the real presence of God. The soul is never less alone than when it is alone with God.

### How to Use the Word in Prayer

It is best to have no book but the Bible, that Scripture may be interpreted by Scripture. I find it well to take the sayings of psalmist and prophet and turn them into prayers. Avoid the lure of sidetracks. I have been interested to find that men known far and wide for their Biblical scholarship always use the Authorized Version in their devotions. I commend their example. Search the Scriptures. The heart is soon aglow when the Word is alight.

The Word of God is like God's world: it is all

interesting and all wonderful, but there are places
to which we go often in thought and affection if
not in actual visits. There are beauty-spots of
which we never tire, and sacred places of hallowed
association. So there are pages of the Bible that
wear thin with use, and some that are stained with
tears. There are favorite Psalms that register the
pilgrimage of the soul. I love the thirty-seventh, the
forty-sixth, the eightieth, and the one hundred and
sixteenth, and many more besides. Usually I read
through the Psalm, and then return for meditation
to a few verses that have appealed to me. How
often I have countered "fret" with "trust" in
Psalm 37, committed my way unto the Lord, and
hummed and prayed through the matchless words,
"O rest in the Lord, and wait patiently for Him";
and my soul rejoices in the assurance that if I delight myself in the Lord, He will give me the desires
of my heart. It is great to take the Lord's own
words and speak them in praise and plead them in
prayer.

The forty-sixth Psalm is just as wonderful, with
its three-fold division of catastrophe, hostility, and
testimony. Then I go back to the first verse, with
its description of God as Refuge, Strength, and
Help. The Refuge is for sanctuary in perils in which
man is utterly helpless. What can he do against a
changing earth, hurtling mountains, and raging
storm? When sudden calamity comes, and the
foundations slip from under our feet, God is our
Refuge. "The eternal God is thy refuge, and underneath are the everlasting arms" Deut. 33:27. Always underneath! Always lower than our deepest
depths! God is also our Strength. There are demands for which we have no might and enemies
against whom we have not strength. "He gives

power to the faint, and to them that have no might He increaseth strength" Isa. 40:29. Immediately the mind is among the heroes of God, and faith rejoices in the assurance of strength that shall be as the day. God is a Help. There are experiences in which we are incomplete. A Helper is near, companionable, encouraging, inspiring, achieving. Could assurance be more complete? No wonder the heart nestles near to God and whispers, "I will trust, and not be afraid" Isa. 12:2.

The Lord of Hosts is with me;
And the God of Jacob is my refuge.

I wonder how often I have prayed through Psalm 116. It was one of God's earliest gifts to me. There is no need to change the pronoun, for there is a personal pronoun in every verse. I love the alternating surge of a sorrow escaped and the triumphant note of thanksgiving, and I linger long over the vows of the redeemed soul. He had been down into the depths. Every kind of trouble seemed to come at once, and greatest of all was his loss of faith in God and man. Deliverance came when he prayed. Praise followed prayer, and praise became a sacrifice of thanksgiving.

"Return unto thy rest, O my soul;
For the Lord hath dealt bountifully with thee.
For Thou hast delivered my soul from death,
Mine eyes from tears,
And my feet from falling.
I will walk before the Lord
In the land of the living."

There are Scriptures that I read at stated seasons. One of my earliest attempts at real Bible study was to try to write out in order the doings and sayings of our Lord in the week of His Passion, and I go over those passages always in the sacred week. There are similar passages for Advent and other festivals of the Christian year. The first thing I do with a new Bible is to mark the passages in John in which our Lord promises the coming of .the Holy Spirit. Those I read always between Easter and Pentecost, and then I find my inner chamber becomes my Lord's Upper Room.

There are three Scriptures that I have read on fixed days of the week for more than forty years. Every Sunday morning I read the fifth chapter of Revelation, and every Sunday night the seventh chapter from verse 9. Why do I do this? Sunday is the great day of my week. I preach other days, but there is only one day in seven that is specially the Lord's Day. It is a day devoted to worship and the ministry of the Word. To me is given the responsibility of intercessor and prophet, teacher and evangelist. I have to represent Christ, preach Christ, plead for Christ. For all this I need the vision of Christ, and nowhere do I find the vision as He is there revealed in the midst of the throne, in the midst of the redeemed, in the midst of the angels, and in the midst of creation. I can face the day after I have beheld His glory, and said Amen, Hallelujah! in His presence. At night I come back to the vision of His ultimate triumph and commit the day unto Him and rest my heart within the veil.

On Monday morning I invariably read Isaiah 41 from verse 8. Monday morning is a difficult time for the prophet-evangelist. Sunday looks somber on Monday. A blue Monday is the devil's chance, so I resolved at the beginning of my ministry that if I had to have a blue Monday I would have it in the middle of the week, and God gave me this Scripture as a protection against the "blues." Perhaps you would like to know how He did it.

It was in my first month out of college. I was in my room on a Monday morning, wrapped in a blanket, for I had a cold and the room was cold. It rained pitilessly all the morning. Just before noon a cab stopped at the door, and H. S. B. Yates, the minister of Leith, was announced. We had only met twice. When I asked how he was, he answered, "I am a worm, and no man." He had the blue Monday so badly that he had taken a cab and come to see me for a change. His church had been crowded the night before for the first time, and Satan taunted and tormented him into sheer terror. I listened with amused amazement. I am not made that way. He asked me what I did when I felt myself a creeping, crawling, contemptible worm? I had just read the forty-first of Isaiah, and I said, "Here is the very chapter for you. It is God's promise to a worm." We read it. We prayed through it, and he went away greatly comforted. Since then I have read it every Monday morning, and I have found it a rare defense against depression, with the result that Monday has been one of my busiest and happiest days. I go through the Bible, as I have gone through these passages of Scripture.

These are intimate words, but at any rate you do not wonder now that to me the Word of the Lord is precious. All the time I have tried to keep in mind the overworked and toil-driven who have little or no space for an inner sanctuary. That is why I urge the Bible as the only necessary book for the devotional hour. For the same reason I advise that it be studied in short portions, lest prayer become secondary in the place consecrated to prayer.

## 6. Praying in the Name

The most incredible things are promised to prayer. The Old Testament abounds in promises and examples. Deliverance and help, guidance and grace were assured to those who called upon God and committed their way unto Him. Nothing was too hard for the Lord, and nothing was impossible to those who prayed. Some of the passages are overwhelming in their challenge to prayer. Here is one: "Thus saith the Lord, the Holy One of Israel, and his Maker: Ask Me of the things that are to come; concerning My sons, and concerning the work of My hands, command ye Me" Isa. 45:11. Prayer passes from entreaty to command.

There is no limit to the possibility of prayer, and the Old Testament confirms and attests the promises by examples and demonstrations of its power. Our Lord speaks with the same illimitable speech. His word is, "Ask, and it shall be given you; seek, and ye shall find; knock, and it shall be opened unto you: for every one that asketh receiveth; and he that seeketh findeth; and to him that knocketh it shall be opened" Matt. 7:7, 8. He gave prayer a new basis, a new confidence, and a new range. For He gave as its reason the fact that God is our heavenly Father. Prayer is a child's petition. "If ye, then, being evil, know how to give good gifts unto your children, how much more shall your Father which is in Heaven give good things to them that ask Him" Matt. 7:11. There is one saying of Jesus that is even more startling than that of Isaiah. "Therefore," says He, "I say unto you, What things soever ye desire, when ye pray, believe that ye receive them, and ye shall have them" Mark 11:24.

### "Whatsoever Ye shall Ask in My Name"

The promise to prayer reaches its climax in the Upper Room on that memorable night of revelation and tragedy. Jesus declared Himself to be the basis of prayer. They were to pray in a new way. They were to pray in His name, and they would be heard for His sake. As there are seven words on the Cross, so there are seven words concerning prayer in the fellowship of the Upper Room. They gather up and complete the whole revelation of the Scriptures, and enlarge and certify the promises of God. It would seem to be sacrilege not to quote them in full, for no other words can compare with them.

"And whatsoever ye shall ask in my name, that will I do, that the Father may be glorified in the Son. If ye shall ask anything in my name, I will do it" John 14:13, 14.

"If ye abide in me, and My words abide in you, ye shall ask what ye will, and it shall be done unto you" John 15:7.

"Ye did not choose me, but I chose you, and appointed you, that ye should go and bear fruit, and that your fruit should abide: that whatsoever ye shall ask of the Father in my name He may give it you" John 15:16.

"And ye therefore now have sorrow: but I will see you again, and your heart shall rejoice, and your joy no one taketh away from you. And in that day ye shall ask me no question (marg. R.V.). Verily, verily, I say unto you, If ye shall ask anything of the Father, He will give it you in my name. Hitherto have ye asked nothing in my name: ask, and ye shall receive, that your joy may be full. . . . In that day ye shall ask in my name" John 16:22-26.

What extraordinary promises these are that are pledged to prayer in the name of our Lord and Saviour Jesus Christ. They abound in universal and unconditional terms. All things, whatsoever ye ask! Prayer reaches its highest level when offered in the name which is above every name, for it lifts the petitioner into unity and identity with Himself.

### "In the Name of Our Lord Jesus Christ"

Our Lord never explained what was meant by praying in His name. The meaning was plain enough to every Israelite. God was in His name. He had made them elect people, that they might be the interpreters, custodians, and witnesses of His name. When they dishonored it in their own land and degraded it among the Gentiles, He redeemed and restored them for the sanctification of the name. "I do not this for your sakes, but for Mine Holy names sake, which ye have profaned among the heathen, whither ye went. And I will sanctify my great name."

Our Lord speaks in terms of Deity. To pray in Christ's name means something more than adding "for Christ's sake" to our petitions. The name expresses personality, character, and Being. The Person is in the name. Prayer in Christ's name is prayer according to the quality of His Person, according to the character of His mind, and according to the purpose of His will. To pray in the name of Christ is to pray as one whose mind is the mind of Christ, whose desires are the desires of Christ, and whose purpose is one with that of Christ.

Such correspondence and identification with Christ secure the balance and interpretation of the promises given to prayer. The absolute and unconditional promises find their relativity and conditions in Him. In the Old Testament prayer was conditioned upon urgency, intensity, and sincerity. God was found of men when they cried unto Him out of a great need; when they sought Him with all their heart, and when there was sincerity of purpose and motive. Men found that God required truth in the innermost soul, and that they were not heard if they regarded iniquity in their hearts, or came to Him with insincere pretences upon their lips. Our Lord demanded importunity and a forgiving spirit of all who prayed. In the prayer in the name all conditions are unified and simplified in Him. Sincerity is tested in the name. Motive is judged in the name. Prayer is proved in the name. Prayer is sanctified in the name. Prayer is endorsed by the name, when it is in harmony with the character, mind, desire, and purpose of the name. That is why in John 15:7 the words of Christ are interchangeable with His name. "If ye abide in me, and my words abide in you, ye shall ask what ye will, and it shall be done unto you." It is something like the word of the Psalmist, "Delight thyself also in the Lord; and He shall give thee the desires of thine heart" 37:4; or that of John, "Beloved, if our heart condemn us not, then have we confidence toward God. And whatsoever we ask, we receive of Him, because we keep His commandments, and do those things that are pleasing in His sight" 1 John 3:21, 22. Prayers offered in the name of Christ are

scrutinized and sanctified by His nature, His purpose, and His will. They are endorsed by Him.

## "For the Sake of the Name"

It means more than that. We are heard for His sake.
He is the petitioner. He ever liveth to make intercession for us. In the Apocalypse He is represented
as taking our prayers and adding to them the fire
of the altar that makes them prevail. He told His
disciples He was going to the Father, and that He
was going to pray on their behalf, and whatever
they asked of the Father in His name the Father
would do it. Not for their own sake, but for His
sake they would be heard.

When I was in Leeds a man came a long way to
look at a factory in which he was interested. He
wrote to the firm, and his request was politely de-
clined. He went to the company and presented his
card. It was returned, and he was refused. No argument could get him beyond the little shutter in the
outer office. He told his disappointment to a
friend, who suggested I might be able to help him.
He came to see me. I gave him my card, and wrote
to the head of the firm. Next day he presented his
request, and handed in my card, and immediately
every door opened to him. His petition was
granted, but not for his own sake. The head of the
firm saw me in him.

In some such way we pray in Christ's name. He
endorses our petitions and makes our prayers His
own, and "the Father hears Him pray." We are not
heard for our much speaking, nor for our loud
shouting. Neither are we heard for our fine phrasing, nor our much weeping. Neither are we heard
for our good works, nor for our self-denials. Prayer
in His name is heard for His name's sake. In the

40  secret sanctuary of the inner chamber we ask, seek, and knock in His Holy name, and present our prayers in the sure confidence of His wonderful and glorious word, "Ye did not choose me, but I chose you, and appointed you . . . that whatsoever ye shall ask of the Father in My name, He may give it you" John 15:16.

"Ask, and ye shall receive" Matt. 7:7.


## 7. Praying in the Spirit

Early in the year 1882 there came to me an experience that lifted my life to a new plane of understanding and of power. The demands of an impossible task awakened me to a sense of need. I had neither power nor might in either service or prayer. I began to pray for power for service, and God led me to the answer by way of equipment for prayer. I thought I knew how to pray and had prayed much over the work to which He had sent me. When I began to seek power, my ears were opened before my eyes began to see.

I heard testimonies to which I had been deaf. Others had been driven to God baffled by lack of power, but they always associated the gift of power with an experience of holiness about which I was not keen. It was power I wanted. I wanted power that I might succeed, and my chief concern for power was the success it would bring. I wanted success that would fill the chapel, save the people, and bring down the strong fortifications of Satan with a crash. I was young, and I was in a hurry. Twelve of us began to pray in band. He led us to Pentecost. It awakened my mind as well as

cleansed my heart. It gave me a new joy and a new
power, a new love and a new compassion. It gave
me a new Bible and a new message. Above all else,
it gave me a new understanding and a new intimacy
in the communion and ministry of prayer; it taught
me to pray in the Spirit.

### The Co-operation of the Spirit

The work of the Holy Spirit is always in co-operation. He never works alone. He depends upon
human co-operation for the mediation of His mind,
the manifestation of His truth and the effectual
working of His will. He indwells the Body of
Christ, as Christ dwelt in the Body prepared for
Him by the Holy Spirit. Revelation came from the
Spirit of Truth as men of God were inspired by
Him. The Word is His, but the writing is with the
hands of men. This two-fold action runs through
the whole of redemption by Christ Jesus. Our Lord
was born of a woman, but conceived by the Holy
Spirit of God. He grew in stature and in knowledge
in the house of Joseph, instructed and guided by
the Holy Spirit. His teaching and ministry were in
the power of the same Spirit. He offered Himself
without blemish unto God through the Eternal
Spirit, and it was the Spirit that raised up Christ
from the dead. There is the same co-operation in
all the experience of salvation. There is always a
human and a divine factor. There is a two-fold witness, a two-fold leading, a two-fold work, and a
two-fold intercession. We pray in the Spirit, and
the Spirit maketh intercession for us.

### The Fellowship of the Spirit in Prayer

The Holy Spirit does nothing of Himself, neither
does He do anything for Himself. His mission is to

glorify Christ, and all He does is based upon the finished work of Christ. He could not be given until Jesus was glorified, and in experience there can be no Pentecost until there is a Coronation. The Spirit is the Coronation gift of Jesus, whom the Father has made to be both Lord and Christ. The fellowship of the Spirit in prayer is made possible by an experience in Christ. The sequence is set forth in the eighth chapter of Romans (verses 9 to 27). Those who pray in the Spirit must be in the Spirit, and if the Spirit of God is to make intercession for us He must dwell in us. If we live after the flesh we die, if we are led of the Spirit, and walk not after the flesh, but after the Spirit, then the Spirit dwells in us, lives through us, and works by us. Then comes to pass that which is written, "And in like manner the Spirit also helpeth our infirmities: for we know not how to pray as we ought; but the Spirit Himself, that dwelleth in us, maketh intercession for us with groanings which cannot be uttered; and He that searcheth the hearts knoweth what is the mind of the Spirit, because He maketh intercession for the saints according to the will of God" Rom. 8:26, 27. The Holy Spirit searches the deep things of God, He takes of the things of Christ and reveals them unto us. God knows the mind of the Spirit; we pray in the Spirit, instructed and inspired by Him, and He makes intercession for us in wordless intercession. That is the New Testament explanation of prayer that prevails. Though I did not know it until years after, that is what happened to me when God gave me a new understanding, a new joy, and a new power in prayer. A new Personality entered a new Temple, and set up a new Altar. As I live, yet not I; so I pray, yet not I. I pray in the Spirit, and the Spirit

## The Spirit Helping Our Infirmities

He instructs and inspires all true prayer. There is no truer word than that "we know not what we should pray for as we ought." There is no realm in which we so soon come to the end of what we know as in that of prayer. Our petitions urge wants that are immediate, obvious, and urgent. We cannot see deep enough or far enough to know what is our real need. Most people would like good health, home comfort, congenial conditions, happy friendships, a little more money, and better success; but who can tell if these would be for their ultimate good? God sees deeper and farther, and He may will otherwise. How often have people who have pleaded with breaking hearts that a life might be spared lived to thank God that the Lord took when He did? He knew what was coming, and took them from the evil to come. The Holy Spirit knows the mind of Christ and the will of God, and He teaches us how to pray and what to pray for. If any man lack wisdom, let him ask of God, and He will give him more than wisdom, He will give Him the Spirit of wisdom to instruct, strengthen, and guide.

The Holy Spirit creates the conditions of prayer. We may ask amiss, not only in what we ask, but also in the reason for asking. He sanctifies desire and directs it into the will of God, so that we desire what God wills to give. That is how it comes to pass that if we delight ourselves in the Lord, we can be sure that He will give us the desires of our heart. We want what He wills. The Spirit brings to expression the unutterable things of the soul. His groanings are before our praying, and our prayers are born of His travail. In Him is the supply of life and desire, wisdom and faith, intercession and power. He quickens desire, purifies motive, inspires confidence, and assures faith.

## The Prayer of the Spirit

This is the inner meaning of prayer. It is more than asking, it is communion, fellowship, co-operation, identification with God the Father and the Son by the Holy Spirit. Prayer is more than words, for it is mightiest when wordless. It is more than asking, for it reaches its highest glory when it adores and asks nothing. When a child entered his father's study and walked up to him at his desk, the father turned and asked, "What did you want, sonny?" The little boy answered, "Nothing, daddy, I just came to be with you."

This mystery of the Spirit is the key to other mysteries. The secret of the Lord is made manifest to those who pray in the fellowship of the Spirit. There are stages of prayer. In one stage we pray and ask Him to help. There is a more wonderful way in which He prays and we assent, and His praying is ours. He makes intercession within the Temple of our hearts, and our Lord ever lives to make intercession for us at the right hand of the Father. The Spirit within our spirits prays, working in us to will and to do the will and good pleasure of our Father which is in Heaven. He is God the Spirit representing God the Father, and God the Son, and the Three are one God. He is the power that worketh in us. He it is that unifies hearts in prayer and makes them an irresistible unity in intercession. The assurance of answered prayer comes from Him, and He it is that makes prayer the mightiest force in the universe of God. The

secret of it all is in Him. The power of it all is by
Him. The joy of it all is with Him. The biggest
thing God ever did for me was to teach me to pray
in the Spirit.

We are never really men of prayer in the best
sense, until we are filled with the Holy Ghost.

Therefore, Lord, teach us to pray in the Spirit!

## 8. Praying to God Our Father

Our Lord bases prayer on personal relationship.
He taught us to call God our Father, and the impli-
cation of sonship changes the whole aspect of
prayer. Whatever difficulties may remain, com-
munication must be possible between father and
child, and to suggest that a child may not ask of a
father would be to empty the terms of all meaning.
It is a child's right to ask, and it is a father's responsibility to hear in affectionate sympathy and
discerning love. The wonder is not that God hears
prayer, but that He is our Father. The greater wonder includes the less. The revelation that God is
Father establishes the possibility and reasonable-
ness of prayer. The one establishes the other. God
would not be Father if His children could not pray.
All the teaching of Jesus about the supremacy of
the child-heart in the Kingdom of God is rank blas-
phemy if God is not our Father. The relationship
carries with it accessibility, intimacy, and fearless
love.

Sons of great men have sometimes remembered
their father as an institution rather than as a father,
and God is to some of His children little more than
an institution. It was not thus that Jesus revealed
Him.

There is no lowering of His majesty in the intimacy of the family relationship. He is still the Holy and Most High God; the High and Lofty One, that inhabits eternity. The Sermon on the Mount, with its relation of God to sparrows and lilies, detracts nothing from the majesty of Isaiah's vision of Him, "The everlasting God, the Lord, the Creator of the ends of the earth." He is still "the King eternal, immortal, invisible, the only wise God . . . the Blessed and Only Potentate, the King of Kings, and Lord of Lords, Who only hath immortality, dwelling in the light which no man can approach unto; Whom no man hath seen, nor can see" 1 Tim. 1:17; 6:15, 16.

There are many such revelations of the Divine glory and majesty, and it is well to ponder them in adoring worship; but Jesus Christ turned them into terms of filial value. He is our Father! That is the crowning fact. To the child He is just Father. Others may cringe in fear, but the child heart is a stranger to terror. I have never forgotten the dread that gripped me when, as a youth, I was invited to go for an interview at the manse. I walked past the door several times before I had courage to ring the bell, and as I stood at the door my heart throbbed in my ears. Imagine my surprise when shown into the room to find the great man on all-fours, giving a ride to riotously happy children, who turned his long beard into driving-reins! He was their father! They knew nothing of the awe in which others stood of him, and as they grew older and knew something of his greatness their reverence deepened, but they were not fearful. The children of the House are free and fearless.

The heavens cannot contain God our Father, but He dwells in the inner chamber of the soul. He is in secret, and sees in secret. He waits and watches for the opening of the sanctuary door. It is holy ground, and must be approached with reverence. The soul must summon all its powers for this its holiest exercise. Communion is deeper than theology. Prayer in secret is life finding expression in the realized Presence of God our Father. All things are voluntarily laid bare before Him. All pretence is stripped from motive, all hypocrisy from desire, all dissimulation from speech. A season of silence is the best preparation for speech with God. Infinite glory finds new value when interpreted in terms of Fatherhood, and prayer finds new horizons in the majesty of our Father in Heaven.

If God be Father we may pray, but if He is such a Father why need we pray?

"When ye pray, use not vain repetitions, as the heathen do: for they think that they shall be heard for their much speaking. Be not ye therefore like unto them: for your Father knoweth what things ye have need of, before ye ask Him" Matt. 6:7, 8. Then what need is there to ask? We do not pray to inform God. Neither do we pray to persuade Him, for His love needs neither to be induced nor coaxed. No father answers his son's prayer for bread with a stone, or the request for a fish with a scorpion. Wisdom and love combine to answer need, and not to make sport of infirmity. "Ask, and it shall be given you; seek, and ye shall find; knock, and it shall be opened unto you. For every one that asketh, receiveth; and he that seeketh, findeth; and to him that knocketh, it shall be opened" Matt. 7:7-8.

It is no part of our purpose to discuss the problems of prayer. We are seeking to learn how to pray, and barren speculations have nothing to teach us. No part of the man must be shut out when the man is shut in. Reason is as truly of God as emotion, and either divorced from the other leaves the soul maimed and incapacitated. Vision comes to love apart from reason, but reason conserves the vision and translates it into life. Our spiritual life stands in knowledge of God, but it is not a knowledge that is acquired or achieved by the energy of flesh and blood. Love is the bond of fellowship in prayer. Attempts to rationalize love damp its fires, but where reason is dethroned, emotion becomes a conflagration. The study and the oratory are allies, but the inner chamber is better to be a place apart; then prayer enlightens thinking, and thinking kindles the altar-fires of the heart.

God as Father is the key to the problem of prayer. God is more than a Creator. He is our Father: heavenly Father, holy Father, righteous Father; the God of love and still the God of law. "The Sabbath was made for man," and the Universe of God was made for the family of God.

### "In the Glory of His Father"

The fact that we pray to God our Father in Heaven tells us much as to how we should pray. The Son of God gloried in the glory of His Father. It was His habit to rise early that He might behold His glory and delight in His presence. He rejoiced in the Father's greatness and in the majesty of His power. It is good to go over His affirmations of the Father. "My Father!" The accents of adoring love vibrate in every tone.

He loved to dwell upon the care and bounty of the Father's love. Nothing is insignificant. Each is to the Infinite as if there were no other. Even the odd sparrow is not forgotten, and man is so much the more the child of His care that even the hairs of his head are numbered. He lived in the sovereign will of the holy and righteous Father. He did not pray to subdue the Father's will to His desire; but that the will of the Father might be done. The sweat and agony of prayer were in the strong praying of the Father's Son, and it was always in obedience to the Father's will.

Because we pray to our Heavenly Father in the secret place of prayer, we may pray with the artless unreserve of little children. There is nothing about which we may not pray. We pray as His children, and we trust Him as our Heavenly Father. His answer will transcend our asking. A true father waits to bless in discretion, as well as in readiness. Sometimes He waits for us. Sometimes the answer is given long before the one who prayed is told, but "every one that asketh, receiveth."

Dr. Adoniram Judson as he lay dying heard of the remarkable answer to his prayer for the Jews when he was a missionary in Burma, and he uttered this testimony, "I never prayed sincerely and earnestly for anything but it came; at some time—no matter how distant the day—somehow, in some shape, probably the last I should have devised, it came."

"When thou prayest, enter into thy inner chamber, and when thou hast shut thy door, pray to thy Father which is in secret" Matt. 6:6.

"UNTO HIM THAT IS ABLE TO DO EXCEEDING ABUNDANTLY ABOVE ALL THAT WE ASK OR THINK" Eph. 3:20.

## 9. The Importunity of Prayer

Our Lord taught men to pray to God as Father. That is the central fact of His teaching. "When ye pray say, Our Father, which art in Heaven" Matt. 6:9. He rebukes all parade and pretence in prayer. It must be in secret and there must be simplicity and sincerity. Hypocrisy cannot live where either much speaking or fine phrasing is forbidden. Fathers and children do not make speeches to each other. Nothing could be simpler, more natural, more assuring. "Ask, and ye shall receive; for every one that asketh receiveth."

### Importunity and Persistence

Alongside this teaching come the parables of the Friend at Midnight and the Unjust Judge. They are not like His other parables, for they teach by contrast, and not by comparison. God is not like the reluctant friend or the unjust judge. Then why tell the stories? The point in common between them and prayer is that in both importunity prevails. If the suppliants were not heard for their much speaking, their persistence had much to do with their prevailing. What place is there for such importunity in the prayers of children to their Heavenly Father?

Our Lord Himself prayed with intensity and importunity. He rose early to pray. He spent all nights in prayer. The Epistle to the Hebrews tells us that He offered up prayers and supplications with strong crying and tears. The awe of

Gethsemane is full of mystery. He called upon God
as Father, but in His praying there was the sweat
and agony of blood. "He kneeled down and
prayed, saying, Father, if Thou be willing, remove
this cup from Me: nevertheless not My will, but
Thine be done . . . and being in an agony He
prayed more earnestly; and His sweat became as it
were great drops of blood falling to the ground"
Luke 22:41-44. Matthew 26:38-46 tells us that He
prayed a third time using the same words. He
wrought many mighty works in nature and in men,
calming the tempest, casting out devils, and raising
the dead, but in none of them is there any trace of
strain or travail. Virture went out of Him and He
wearied in toil, but there was the ease of mastery
in all He did; but of His praying it is said, "As He
prayed He sweat." He prayed in an agony unto
blood. If God be Father, why such agony in the
praying of His Son?

## "Prayer and Supplication"

In the parable of the reluctant friend, the man was
prepared to entreat till his request was granted.
This is not much like praying to a Heavenly Father.
God is not like that, but praying that prevails is
like that. The same is true of the Parable of the
Unjust Judge. God is not like him, but prayer
pleads and persists until it prevails. Petition asks,
supplication entreats, pleading argues.

Job asks for an opportunity to plead his cause,
"Oh that I knew where I might find Him, that I
might come even to His seat! I would order my
cause before Him, and fill my mouth with argu-
ments. I would know the words which He would
answer me, and understand what He would say
unto me" Job 23:3-5. God invites to reason, and

prayer is given the right to plead, but if God be Father, knowing what we need, waiting to be asked, why should there be supplication and pleading?

## Striving and Wrestling

When Peter was in prison "Prayer was made without ceasing of the Church unto God for him" Acts 12:5. The Revised Version substitutes "earnestly" for "without ceasing." They continued earnestly in prayer. They prayed all night, and kept on praying until the answer came. There was the same contending in the prayer of the Syro-Phoenician woman. She came to grips and held on till Jesus commended her faith and granted her request.

Striving is a familiar word in the New Testament. Paul exhorts the Christians in Rome "by our Lord Jesus Christ, and by the love of the Spirit, that ye strive together with me in your prayers to God for me" Rom. 15:30. He commends Epaphras as a praying pastor who strove and labored in prayer Col. 4:12, and tells the Colossians how greatly he himself strove for them. Prayer is work that involves contending, a toil that implies labor; but why should it be a toil and a labor?

Even the idea of wrestling is associated with prayer. It is not suggested that we wrestle with God, but there is a grappling that calls for vigilance and concentration. It is quite clear that prayer is not the easy thing that seems to be implied in the simplicity of asking our Heavenly Father for what we want and getting it. There is travail in it. There is work in it. There is entreaty in it. There is importunity in it. Maybe Coleridge was not far wrong when he spoke of prayer as the highest energy of which the human heart is capable and the greatest

## The Paradox of Prayer

Prayer is full of apparent contradictions. It is so simple that a child can pray, and it is so profound that the wisest cannot explain its mystery. It is so easy that those who have no strength can pray, and it is so strenuous that it taxes every resource of energy, intelligence, and power. It is so natural that it need not be taught, and it is so far beyond nature that it cannot be learned in the school of this world's wisdom. Prayer is a world in itself, and no one aspect of life's similes can explain it. The relation of Father and child has bigger meanings in Revealed Truth than in our modern conception. Jesus spoke of Him as the Heavenly, the Holy, and the Righteous Father. Peter combines in Him both Father and Judge. The modern mind resents prayer that is an agony and entreaty, a pleading and striving, a wrestling and persistence. That is not the way parents would like to see their children come to them, and so they reason it is not the way for them to pray.

For many years I kept by me a check on the Bank of Heaven. It was sent to me one Christmas from America by Dr. A. T. Pierson. It was made payable to bearer, and promised to deliver on demand whatever I might need. On the face of it was the text, "My God shall supply all your need, according to His riches in glory by Christ Jesus our Lord" Phil. 4:19. Prayer is just cashing checks! Is it as simple as that? Is God at the counter waiting to hand over whatever we ask? Experience soon disillusions those who think that is the whole of prayer. If that were all, why should there be a secret place and a closed door?

Fatherhood implies sonship, and sonship involves correspondence of nature, character, and mind. The Holy Father is the Father of holy sons. He is in secret, and we are in secret. To be shut in alone with God is to be at the Judgment Seat. "If I regard iniquity in my heart," said the Psalmist, "the Lord will not hear me." We cannot pray so long as our hearts condemn us. God does not give orders, any more than He supplies them. He talks with His children and encourages them to reason with Him. He waits to bless, not only in readiness, but with discretion.

Prayer is a discipline and an education. Jesus spake Divine wisdom when He forbade us to cast pearls before swine: it is contrary to the Divine order. Intensity is a law of prayer. God is found of those who seek Him with all their heart. Wrestling prayer prevails. The fervent effectual prayer of the righteous is of great force. God hates strange fire. We must never try to work up an emotion of intensity. Avoid all that is mechanical and perfunctory. Shun the casual and flippant. Suspect all easy and cheap methods like that of the bank and the store. Leave all directors and prompters to the place of corporate and liturgical prayer. When alone with God, be alone with Him. Begin in silence. Speak with simplicity. Listen in meekness. Never leave without a conscious season of real communion. We have not to persuade God, but He has to discipline and prepare us. In all moods and at all seasons pour out the soul in prayer and supplication with thanksgiving, and if the Spirit groans in intercession do not be afraid of the agony of prayer. There are blessings of the Kingdom that are only yielded to the violence of the vehement soul.

A minister told of his Sunday School teacher
who despaired of his class and asked to be released.
The Superintendent persuaded him to try again,
and to promise that every day for three months he
would pray in secret, for every boy. Every boy in
the class was saved, and four of them became min-
isters of great usefulness and power.

## 10. The Recompense of Prayer

"Thy Father which seeth in secret shall recompense thee" Matt. 6:6. Our Lord did not hesitate
to associate recompense with prayer, and who can
measure the blessings that come through the ave-
nue of prayer? Those who deny that prayer
changes things, or effects any wonders of deliverance and help, are among the first to exalt its influence on the soul that prays. The value of a daily
habit of withdrawal and hallowed seclusion is
beyond exaggeration. The contemplation of the
unseen, the attempt to think in terms of the eternal, and the honest endeavor of the soul to enter
in communion with God, in themselves redeem life
from all that is fitful, fretful and futile. Apart from
specific blessings, the sheer influence of a daily
habit of private prayer is incalculable. I propose to
consider three, maybe four, examples.

It has been said that the mountains of the Bible
will repay the climber, and no life is richer in
mountain scenes than that of Moses. For forty
years he had wandered among their solitary
heights, feeding his flock and grappling with the
great problems of his people and their God. He had

been schooled in all the learning of the Egyptians, but when God wanted to instruct him, He took him from the valley into the mount. It was amid the silence of the everlasting hills the polished courtier and distinguished scholar was fitted for the work of delivering and guiding the people of God. His service began and ended in the Mount. On the eve of every new development, and on every critical occasion, God called him, and he went up. Whenever the burden of his charge oppressed him, he hastened to seek God in the Mount. What he found in those ascents is still the wonder of the world.

The Mount of God was a privileged place of peculiar sanctity. God had commanded that it should be fenced, lest the cattle should trample it. "Set bounds about the mount and sanctify it" Ex. 19:23. The people were not permitted to approach. Even priests and elders must stop at the boundary. No companionship was allowed. The most trusted and intimate had to be left to tarry while the servant of God went alone into the Holy Place. The Lord commanded him to get ready and come up early in the morning. God wants man at his best. All these instructions of the Pentateuch anticipate the Sermon on the Mount. There is a very special sense in which God dwells in the secret place. He is in secret: He sees in secret. God wants us in the Mount. Come away! Come up! Come up early! Before daybreak Jesus and Moses were alone with God. Let us go up with Moses, that we may learn what he found in the Mount of God.

### The Place of Revelation
### Moses found God in the Mount

Read the story in the third chapter of Exodus.

After forty years of exile for his championship of God's people, the shepherd-prince found the God of Israel. He was not a stranger to Him in Egypt. He had renounced the privileges and pleasures of a royal palace and cast in his lot with the afflicted people of his race. He had given proof of his zeal for the Most High, but he had never had a personal revelation of Him till he found Him that day in the Mount. There is much outer-court service in the Lord's temple. Many serve and suffer for Him who never enter the Holy Place where the Most High dwells between the cherubim. It is there He reveals Himself as nowhere else. He manifests Himself to those who pray in secret as He cannot to those who have no inner sanctuary of the soul.

### Moses found himself where he found his God

It was not a pleasant discovery; it seldom is. He was a disappointed reformer. He had made great sacrifices for Israel, and he found them resentful of his interference, jealous of his motives, distrustful of his purpose. For forty years he had brooded over a wicked king, a spiritless and ungrateful people. He nursed his grievance with the resignation of a martyr and the despondency of a disappointed leader. "Put thy hand in thy bosom," commanded the Voice out of the fire; and, lo, it was leprous, white as snow! That was a startling surprise for him. He had thought the other people were leprous, but neither his own heart nor hands were clean. That is the kind of discovery men make in the Mount of God, and that is one reason we are so reluctant to ascend. He discovered other things besides leprosy. He found himself. He found latent powers. He found his vocation. He found that a stick he had carried daily was a symbol and instrument of Divine power. We discover ourselves when God reveals Himself to us.

### Moses found the Will of God in the Mount

It was there he received the law. After forty days alone with God he brought heaven's laws to earth on two tables of stone. Those laws remain to this day the foundation of all righteous government among men. After centuries of progress they are still the basis of civilization.

He not only received the Commandments which were to be the cornerstones of good government for all time; he also received directions concerning local and personal details. See the minute instructions for the building of the Tabernacle. No trifle is overlooked. Nails and fringes, tongs and snuffers are all included. Every detail was designed in the Mount. Every pattern was divinely fixed and approved. The way to the Mount is still open. The Divine pattern of each life is still to be seen in the secret place of the Most high God. The humblest follower of Jesus may know the Divine will at first hand. It is every man's privilege to be fully assured in the will of God. The Divine attention to detail is amazing. Nothing is too trivial for Omniscience. Come straight to God. Do not bother other people. Lay all questions naked before Him, and He will make it plain to you what is His will. When God speaks, His speech is easily understood. All questions of the plain should be settled in the Mount, and where there is certainty in the Mount there will be victory on the levels and in the valleys.

### The Place of Power

There is a wonderful story in Exodus 17. It was Israel's first battle. The Amalekites came against

them in Rephidim. Joshua commanded the hosts
of Israel, and Moses went up into the Mount to pray. The fluctuations of the battle were astonishing. In turns the opposing hosts prevailed, until it was found that the issue of the battle was not with the fighters in the field, but with the intercessors in the Mount. It was the weaponless hand of prayer that ruled the battle. "And it came to pass, when Moses held up his hand, that Israel prevailed: and when he let down his hand, Amalek prevailed." Is it necessary to point the moral of the tale? Power is the recompense of prayer. It takes us long to learn that prayer is more important than organization, more powerful than armies, more influential than wealth, and mightier than all learning. Prevailing prayer makes men invincible. They who prevail in the secret place of the Most High cannot be beaten anywhere. All things are possible through secret prayer.

### The Place of Fellowship

In the Mount the Lord spoke unto Moses face to face, as a man speaks to his friend. Like Abraham, Moses was admitted to the friendship of God. He did not come simply to plead petitions and receive orders. He was there for communion on a common basis of fellowship. The inner chamber is an audience chamber where the soul enters into friendly intercourse and mutual interchange. It is a place for listening as well as for speech. The most important part of prayer is not what we say to God, but what God says to us. It is no place for hurry. The soul must be still and wait before the Lord.

The Mount is the place of intercession. There is a moving story in Exodus 32:9-14 of how Moses pleaded for Israel. He stepped into the breach. God looks for men who will stand in the gap Ezek. 22:30. God encourages us to speak for others and to plead for them. He suffers entreaty. How daring was Abraham's faith! With what audacity Moses stepped into the breach and urged the plea for Israel! With what passion Paul pleaded for his kinsmen according to the flesh! We are commanded to pray for one another, and who can tell what blessings come to men through intercession?

It was in the Mount Moses saw God's glory. It is a vision of the secret place. It was in the Mount Jesus was transfigured. The glory seen is also shared. Prayer transfigures. Moses came down from the Mount all aglow with the glory, but "he wist not that the skin of his face shone." That is the secret of radiant humility. "As Jesus prayed, He was transfigured before them" Luke 9:29. Glory is the recompense of prayer. The Lord who calls His servant into the Mount sends him down. Peter wanted to stay. We go up that we may go down. We enter in that we may come out. There are golden images, senseless and wicked passions, enslaved and misguided people, distracted fathers and devil-torn sons and daughters that need the vision and the power of God. Come up! Go down! God wants us in the Mount and He wants us in the valley. Moses died in the Mount. Those who go up and down at God's bidding are sure to end in going up to come down no more.


## 11. The Power of Prayer

Elijah is chosen in the New Testament as the example of prayer. There were many others in the Old Testament Scriptures who called upon God

and were mightily delivered. Jacob so prayed that
his name was changed from Jacob to Israel. Moses
was preeminently a man of prayer; he was sustained, guided, and transformed by prayer. Daniel
prayed habitually and his life was a romance of
prayer. There were others, from Abraham to the
last of the Old Testament prophets, including kings
and priests, soldiers and reformers, widows and suf-
ferers. Why was Elijah chosen from among them
all?

## A Mighty Man

Elijah occupies a larger place in the New Testament
than in the Old, and it is always an advantage when
the New Testament gives the interpretation of an
Old Testament theme. The Old Testament story
offers no explanation of the prophet's power. His
ministry consisted in a series of dramatic appear-
ances, and the most sensational event in a sensational life was its dramatic end. For the most part
he dwelt in solitary places, and he was always a
solitary figure. "I alone," was a plaint often on his
lips. The Old Testament closes with a promise of
his return, and the New Testament opens with the
record of its fulfilment. He championed God,
defied kings, and held the destiny of nations in his
hand.

The New Testament explanation of the man and
his work is that he was a man of prayer. On the
face of the Old Testament story, prayer was an
outstanding feature of this man, but according to
the New Testament, prayer was the entire explanation of the man and his marvellous doings. That he
was a mountain of a man is plain for all to see, but
he was a man of like passions with other men, and
whatever difference there was between him and

62 others was due to prayer. James says, "Elijah was a man of like passions with us, and he prayed"—that is what made him different. Prayer accounts for the man, as it accounts for Abraham and Jacob, David and Daniel, but there was something in Elijah's praying that gave distinction even among saints mighty in prayer. What was it? Why did Jehovah come to be known as the Lord God of Elijah?

## Miracles of Power

The praying of Elijah is a demonstration of the supernatural power of prayer. His prayers were miracles of power. That is what the New Testament says of them. There has always been difficulty with the translation of James 5:16.

The Authorized Version reads:

"The effectual fervent prayer of a righteous man availeth much."

The Revised Version:

"The supplication of a righteous man availeth much in its working."

Dr. Rendel Harris translates it:

"The energized prayer of a righteous man is of great force."

Prayer with Elijah was force, supernatural power, miraculous in its working. He never discussed natural law, and he never doubted supernatural power. He prayed, and there was no rain, and when he prayed for rain, it came in floods. He prayed for life to come again to the dead child of the widow with whom he lodged, and the soul of the child returned. He prayed for fire from heaven, and it fell as he prayed. He did not argue about prayer. He prayed. Praying solves problems of prayer.

There always have been problems about prayer.
In the wilderness they questioned God's power to
transcend known laws of His world. Can God? The
answer of faith turns the question into an affirma-
tion and believes God can. These are hardly the
days in which it is safe to say that anything is
impossible. We stand on the threshold of unex-
plored worlds, and if so much that was incredible
has become possible to man, who shall say that
anything is impossible to God? He who made the
heavens and earth must be bigger than His worlds,
and it is impossible He should be imprisoned within His own laws. The prayer of faith links man's
petition to the power of God. All men believe in
the power of prayer to influence mind, develop
character, and sanctify motive and will, but that is
not all. Prayer changes things. The Lord God of
Elijah had sovereign and omnipotent power, and
these were at the command of the prayer of faith.
Every praying man knows of answers to prayer to
which there is no explanation but in God. I am
reluctant to quote examples, but in my own life
they abound, and the language of Psalm 116 is
often on my lips:
"I love the Lord, because He hath heard
 My voice and my supplications.
 Because He hath inclined His ear unto me,
 Therefore will I call upon Him as long as I live."
   There is one remarkable instance that I cherish
because of the way the story came to me. There
are two buildings in the city of Bristol which are
monuments of answered prayer. One is Muller's
Orphanage, and of the other I am not at present at
liberty to speak. Dr. A. T. Pierson was my friend,
and he was the friend and biographer of Muller. It
was from him I got the first half of the story. He

**64** told me of an occasion when he was the guest of Muller at the orphanage. One night when all the household had retired he asked Pierson to join him in prayer. He told him that there was absolutely nothing in the house for next morning's breakfast. My friend tried to remonstrate with him and to remind him that all the stores were closed. Muller knew all that. He had prayed as he always prayed, and he never told anyone but God of his needs. They prayed. At least Muller did, and Pierson tried to. They went to bed and slept, and breakfast for two thousand children was there in abundance at the usual breakfast hour. Neither Muller nor Pierson ever knew how the answer came. The story was told next morning to Simon Short of Bristol, under pledge of secrecy till the benefactor died. The details of it are thrilling, but all that need be told here is that the Lord called him out of bed in the middle of the night to send breakfast to Muller's Orphanage, and knowing nothing of the need, or of the two men at prayer, he sent provisions that would feed them for a month. That is like the Lord God of Elijah, and still more like the God and Father of our Lord Jesus Christ.

### The Greatest Force on Earth

It is not every kind of praying that works such wonders. It takes a man of prayer to pray as Elijah and George Muller prayed. It is the energized prayer of the righteous man that is of great force. The widow knew that Elijah was a man of God when he prayed her boy back to life 1 Kings 17:24. It is always the crowning proof and the ultimate test. Nothing would turn a nation back to God so surely and so quickly as a Church that prays and prevails. The world will never believe in a religion in which there is no supernatural power. A rationalized faith, a socialized Church, and a moralized Gospel may gain applause, but they awaken no conviction and win no converts.

There is passion in praying that prevails. There was passion in all Elijah did. God loves a man aflame. He cannot abide the lukewarm. He never keeps hot hearts waiting. "Then will I be found of you when ye seek Me with all your hearts" Jer. 29:13. When Elijah prayed, he prayed in his prayer. The praying man was in his petition. It is always the same: Abraham pleading for Sodom, Jacob wrestling in the stillness of the night, Moses standing in the breach, Hannah intoxicated with sorrow, David heart-broken with remorse and grief, Jesus in a sweat of blood. Add to the list from the records of the Church, personal observation and experience. There is no power like that of prevailing prayer. It turns ordinary mortals into men of power. It brings power. It brings fire. It brings rain. It brings life. It brings God.

Recent correspondence has brought me many stories of answered prayer. I can quite understand why critical minds have misgivings as to their evidential value. The man who has not travailed through the supplication is always free to look for other explanations, but to the man who has prayed, the explanation adds to the wonder of the answer. He had the answer before the answer came.

Take one example. A man tells me of a great anxiety in his business life. Like Jehoshaphat, he had no resources to meet the need, but he continued earnestly in prayer to God until one day there came a great peace into his soul and he knew that he was heard. The conditions were unchanged, but he had an assurance of peace, and in a most unexpected way, by a comparatively unknown person, deliverance came. The explanation was obvious, but the answer was no less sure.

It always seems to me quite useless to argue about prayer; a challenge like that of Huxley is utterly futile. The proof that God answers prayer is in praying. I once answered a streetcorner challenge to prove that God answers prayer by challenging the man to come and kneel down and pray, but the challenge was not accepted. I still hold that to be the only way, and that way is scientific and conclusive.

Another story that I may repeat comes from the Rev. T. A. Turney. He was a student in the school where the teacher was both teacher and uncle. He taught by making his students find out things for themselves. He was harder on his nephew than the rest, lest he should be suspected of favoritism. The boy came to the deadlock that awaits us all at some stage of learning. He could not do a problem in mathematics. Day after day he brought it to the teacher, only to be sent back to try again. When this had gone on for more than a week, the boy went one night to a mission service and gave his heart to God. At the communion rail he began to pray. When he got home he turned again to his problem, with the same old result. When he knelt to pray he asked God to help him with this problem. In the night, asleep or awake he does not know, he saw the problem worked out. He got up and wrote it down. Next morning he took it to the teacher, who answered sharply, "Right! Who showed you?"

"God," answered the boy.

### An Energized Intercessor

Have you ever heard of "Praying Hyde"?

The recorded answers to prayer are the least part of his record. He prayed the Indian Keswick into existence. He prayed thousands into the Kingdom of God and hundreds of laborers into the harvest fields of God. Above and beyond all this he prayed himself into the mystery of fellowship in our Lord's intercession. The secret of his prayer-life is that it was a life of prayer.

He was in England in 1911. He went to a mission service where Wilbur Chapman and Charlie Alexander were having a hard time. He took the burden of the mission upon his heart and prayed till victory came. Dr. Chapman asked Mr. Hyde to pray for him, and this is his account of what happened:

"He came to my room, turned the key in the door, dropped on his knees, waited five minutes without a single syllable coming from his lips. I could hear my own heart thumping and his beating. I felt the tears running down my face. I knew I was with God. Then with upturned face, down which the tears were streaming, he said: 'Oh, God!' Then for five minutes at least he was still again, and then, when he knew he was talking with God, his arm went around my shoulder, and there came up from the depth of his heart such petitions for men as I had never heard before. I rose from my knees to know what real prayer was. We believe that prayer is mighty, and we believe it as we never did before."

I am aware that such records of prayer-life may

discourage where they were meant to inspire. I am not asking that you and I should be fashioned after the pattern of exceptional men, but I do rejoice that whatever was given to one is available for all.

## 12. Praying and the Commonplace

Moses and Elijah were not ordinary men. They were so unusual that they were chosen from among all the Old Testament saints to come and talk with Jesus on the Mount of Transfiguration. One was the leader of the Old Covenant, and the other was the most dramatic of its prophets. The rod of Moses and the mantle of Elijah were symbols and instruments of power. Their prayers were miracles. They moved in the realm of the infinite. They controlled the heavens and commanded the earth. Greater than these works of power were the results of prayer in illumination and guidance. God revealed His mind and gave instructions as to His will. In answer to prayer there came the revelation that was beyond human wisdom, and the miracle of the mind was greater than those of material power.

### Prayer and Ordinary Folk

The dramatic stories of prevailing prayer in the Bible have made a profound impression upon the minds of ordinary people. It has standardized miracle as the normal working power of prayer. It is the true standard, for all prayer is supernatural in its working, but it has its discouraging influence. What is the place and work of prayer in the life of ordinary people? What about the people in whose life there is no opportunity for either privacy or leisure, and whose duties are an unrelieved monotony of mechanical commonplace? Is prayer for exceptional people and exceptional circumstances? Or has it a place and a work in lives of ordinary gifts and commonplace living?

Of the New Testament successor of Elijah it is said that he did no miracle. He was not less a man of prayer than his Old Testament predecessor, but food did not multiply at his touch, he raised no dead, and neither water nor fire was at his command. The only miracles in him were in personality, in discernment, and in truth. So we find that supernatural power may work along normal lines of natural law. Ordinary people may pray about commonplace things, and the answer to their prayers may be in an enlightened mind, a triumphant soul, a steadfast faith, and a holy life. There may be no miraculous incidents, but prayer lifts the lowliest and most ordinary life to the exalted plane of the supernatural, and that is the greatest miracle of all.

### Prayer and Daily Toil

We cannot all be Elijahs or Elishas, Abrahams or Daniels, George Mullers or Hudson Taylors, Barnardos or "Praying Hydes," but we can be men and women of prayer. There are praying ones in the Scriptures of whom no miracles are told. They moved in other spheres. They were workers in the workshop of the world. Jacob and Moses were keepers of sheep, with ample spaces of solitude in which to pray. We are not told that Elijah ever worked at anything but prayer.

The example of Elijah's miraculous record needs

to be balanced by that of others who lived and worked among the normal conditions of life. It is expected that preachers and prophets should give themselves to the Word of God and prayer, but what about the man whose life is lived in the factory, the office, or the store? Nehemiah was as truly a man of prayer as Elijah. He was the builder of the wall of Jerusalem. He wrought no miracle, he saw no vision, he had no special commission from Heaven. He never said God had sent him, neither did he ask anyone else to say it for him. A need and an opportunity called him. That was enough. There was a condition that filled his soul with grief, a great work to be done, and no one seeming to care about it. So he prayed. He prayed over the evil tidings, prayed for the ruined city, prayed about the reproach of the people of God, prayed on behalf of those in distress; prayed till his heart was near breaking. Nothing extraordinary happened. No angel came. God gave no sign. When Elijah prayed, things happened. Nehemiah prayed, and nothing happened! Oh, yes, there did! Something happened in Nehemiah, and a miracle in personality is greater than a miracle in nature. Emotion turned to prayer, and prayer turned to conviction; then conviction generated purpose, and purpose directed energy; then energy vitalized activity, until the two sayings come together:

*"SO I PRAYED" and*

*SO WE BUILT."*

Nehemiah's prayers wrought no startling and dramatic manifestation of supernatural power, but it built the wall and restored the city, and in the will of God that was his work. Nehemiah prayed about his work. Prayer was the maintained attitude and continued habit of his life. There are those who reserve prayer for special and desperate occasions. We read of some who prayed because they were at their wits' end. Most people pray then. Some pray under the stress of an emotional mood. Nehemiah prayed all the time, all the way through, and about everything. It was so entirely his habit to pray that he became a man of prayer.

## The Practical Value of Prayer

The habit of prayer implies a certain attitude of life. It predicates God, and recognizes His sovereignty over all. It submits all things to His will, rehearses all things in His presence, judges all things by His standard of values, and lives by faith in Him. Prayer is the essence and test of the godly life. Who can measure its influence upon mind and character, or estimate its value in practical wisdom and dexterous skill?

The Book of Nehemiah is in the Bible, and therein it is written for all to see what prayer did for this man of prayer, who built the wall against tremendous odds. It gave him the commission and cooperation of the King, and secured him all necessary supplies. It brought him courage and sense in dealing with critics and adversaries, and it instructed him in wisdom in adjusting difficulties of labor and wages. It saved him from the tricky craft of the official, and gave him sagacity to resist the cunning of the enemy. It gave him sanctuary when they invented lies and slanders about him. It armed him with faith and humor as well as with a sword and trowel. He kept his hands clean, his wits alert, his courage bright, and prayed his way through. He was sure of God: sure of the character of God, the Word of God, the covenant of God.

We may pray about anything, but prayer will not avail if it is a mere whim or an idle wish. Nehemiah prayed over his work, but he made it his business to know all about the things of which he prayed. His work prospered because he worked at his work. It is no use to pray about work and then neglect it, or play the fool in it, for lack of courage, efficiency, and sense. He prayed and used his wits. He knew the Lord would send supplies; but he took care to have the King's letters. He knew the Lord would protect; but he added a sword to the equipment of the builder's trowel.

Prayer gives vision in the secret place, intelligence in work, sense in judgment, courage in temptation, tenacity in adversity, and a joyous assurance in the will of God. A weaver who prayed over his work, as Nehemiah prayed over his, came to be known as the man who wove every yard of cloth for the Lord Jesus Christ. He never made a fortune, but his work prospered, and his character was of rare worth. Every task and every duty may be sanctified in the word of God and in prayer. The prayer-life in which there are no miracles may be the greatest miracle of all.

There is nothing about which I do not pray. I go over all my life in the presence of God. All my problems are solved there. All questions of liberty as well as duty are settled there. I seek counsel of God, and submit all things to the judgment of God. The sanctuary of my soul is there.

I stood in my study window this morning and watched a gorgeous rainbow come up over the hill. It rose until it stood like a thing apart, and then it moved toward us till one end appeared to rest in

the village and the other in the river. Its colors
were indescribably beautiful, and it filled all the
landscape with its glory. The fields and the trees
reflected the splendor of the heavens. Every common stick and stone was transformed into a thing
of radiant beauty.

So prayer sanctifies and glorifies the commonplace life of ordinary folk.

## 13. The Prayer of Faith

"He that cometh to God must believe that He is,
and that He is a rewarder of them that diligently
seek Him" Heb. 11:6. Faith is necessary to prayer.
Atheists do not pray. God makes faith the first
requisite of prayer, the sole condition of salvation,
the one essential of spiritual life, and the universal
law of power. It is a shallow interpretation of faith
that sneers at salvation by grace through faith
alone. Faith is enough. Faith is all God asks. Faith
is all Jesus asks, "Ye believe in God, believe also in
Me" John 14:1. When the ruler of the synagogue
was told that his daughter was dead, Jesus steadied
his faith, saying, "Fear not: only believe", and
when the distraught father of the demoniac boy
cried out against his own despair, our Lord assured
him that "all things are possible to him that be-
lieveth." Without faith it is impossible to please
God. Without faith it is impossible to pray to God.
Without faith it is impossible to have fellowship
with God. Without faith man can do nothing with
God, and God can do nothing with man. Neither
can man do anything with man apart from faith,
for faith is the basis of civilization as well as of
salvation.

Paul expounds the law of faith in relation to grace, and James expounds the same law in the realm of prayer. There is no controversy between them. Faith to both is more than an intellectual conviction, however sincere. It is a moral and spiritual attitude that commits the whole being to accepted and assured truth. Faith is more than belief. The devils believe and tremble, but they do not trust. Faith is trust. It is not an opinion, not a fiction, not a supposition. It is a faculty of vision, a process of verification, an assurance of knowledge, a logic of life. It demands an honest and impartial mind, a pure and disinterested motive, a loyal and steadfast obedience. This is the faith that works by law to the justification of the ungodly, the sanctification of the unholy, and to the mighty power that prevails in prayer.

"For verily I say unto you, If ye have faith as a grain of mustard seed, ye shall say unto this mountain, Remove hence to yonder place: and it shall remove; and nothing shall be impossible unto you. Howbeit this kind goeth not out but by prayer and fasting" Matt. 17:20, 21. The saying in Matthew's Gospel must be put alongside that in Mark. "Have faith in God. For verily I say unto you, That whosoever shall say unto this mountain, Be thou removed, and be thou cast into the sea; and shall not doubt in his heart, but shall believe that those things which he saith shall come to pass, he shall have whatsoever he saith. Therefore I say unto you, What things soever ye desire, when ye pray, believe that ye receive them, and ye shall have them" 11:22-24.

### The Law of Faith in Prayer

1. *Ask* James 1:5.

The teaching of James consists chiefly of amplifications and applications of our Lord's teaching in the Sermon on the Mount. He begins where our Lord began on the subject of prayer with the simple command to ask, "If any man lack, let him ask of God." The reach of the privilege of asking covers the man's whole need as well as his lack of wisdom. God gives to all that ask, liberally and without upbraiding, therefore "ask, and ye shall receive." There is no limit to the range of prayer. "Whatsoever" is promised to "whosoever," and the largest liberty is given to those who pray. "In nothing be anxious; but in everything by prayer and supplication with thanksgiving let your requests be made known unto God" Phil. 4:6. "Ask, and ye shall receive" John 16:23, 24. Prayer is asking. "Your Heavenly Father knoweth what things ye have need of, before ye ask Him. After this manner therefore pray ye" Matt. 6:8, 9. Why pray if He knows? Because asking is something different from giving information. God waits to be asked, before He gives the gifts that supply man's deepest needs.

2. *Ask in Faith* James 1:6.

Faith is explained by its opposite. Doubt is double-minded and unstable. Like a troubled sea, it is driven by the force of the wind and tossed by the surge of the deep; it is at the mercy of a double motion of oscillation and undulation. Internal conditions disturb, and external circumstances drive. Such a man gets nothing because he is not of one mind, and a two-minded man is unstable in all his ways.

*Ships go East and ships go West,*
*Whatever the winds that blow;*
*The set of the sail, and not the gale,*
*Settles the way we go.*

### 3. *Ask Aright* James 4:3.

It is possible to ask amiss. "Ye ask, and receive not, because ye ask amiss, that ye may spend it in your pleasures." God takes account, not only of what we want, but of why we want it. He looks at the heart. There are some people to whom He will not give audience. Sin shuts men out. "If I regard iniquity in my heart, the Lord will not hear me" Ps. 66:18. Unbelief shuts men out Heb. 4:19; 11:6. An unforgiving spirit shuts men out Matt. 5:23, 24; 6:14, 15; Mark 11:25, 26. An unstable mind shuts men out James 1:7. A condemning conscience shuts men out John 4:14. A self-seeking motive shuts men out James 4:3. Faith works in those who pray that they may ask aright.

### 4. *Ask Righteously* James 5:13-18.

The rightness of the asking goes down to the rightness of the asker. The person who prays is the prayer. He is both the petitioner and the petition; the pleader and the plea; the request and the reason. Patriarchs and Psalmists fall back on their integrity as an argument with God, and their plea is admitted. The alms and prayers of Cornelius were accepted of God, and Peter declared his new faith in these terms: "Of a truth I perceive that God is no respecter of persons: but in every nation he that feareth Him and worketh righteousness is acceptable to Him" Acts 10:34, 35.

It is the praying of the righteous man that is of great force. Faith is no substitute for right living. It does not cover sin; only blood can do that. It saves from sin, gives victory over sin, and makes men righteous with the righteousness of God. There is no condemnation, but an assurance in the will of God that gives "boldness toward God: and whatsoever we ask, we receive of Him, because we keep His commandments, and do those things that are pleasing in His sight" 1 John 3:21, 22.

## 5. *Ask Earnestly.*

God promises to be found of us when we seek Him with all our hearts Jer. 29:13. Elijah's prevailing prayer was intense in its passion. Our Lord's Parables on Prayer emphasize an importunity that persists and insists in spite of discouragement, and the Epistle to the Hebrews speaks of His own praying with strong cries and tears. It is the impassioned prayer that prevails.

## 6. *Ask in the Spirit.*

The prevailing prayer of Elijah was energized prayer. It was inspired, instructed, and empowered of the Holy Spirit.

## 7. *Ask in the Prayer of Faith.*

Ask believingly according to the law of faith. The principle is stated in Mark 11:24, and illustrations are in all the Scriptures. The Honors Roll of Faith in Hebrews 11 furnishes illustrious examples of its power, and in verse 13 there is a picturesque description of its method. Like the man in the Gospels who believed the word that Jesus spake and went his way John 4:50, so these had witness borne to them, and they dared and endured by faith, even dying believing. Israel shouted before the walls of Jericho before there was even a crack in the solid masonry, and the shout of faith brought them down so that there was not a yard of solid masonry left. Jehoshaphat's singers chanted the song of victory before the battlefield was reached, and the song of faith was mightier than thousands of armed men skilled in war. Elijah's promise to the widow was made in the midst of famine, and in the house of faith there was no lack. The prayer of faith works mightily, for it is mighty with the power of God.

"When ye pray, believe that ye have received, and ye shall have."

## 14. Praying "One for Another"

The praying people of the Bible are intercessors. Abraham pleaded for Sodom and Gomorrah. Moses made intercession for apostate Israel. Samuel prayed all night for Saul and continually for the nation. David entreated God for his people. Daniel prayed for the deliverance of the Lord's people from Babylon. Christ prayed for His disciples, and made special intercession for Peter. Paul was an example of his own exhortation "that supplications, prayers, intercessions, thanksgivings be made for all men" 1 Tim. 2:1.

The one thing that is said to have surprised God is that the voice of intercession had ceased. "And He saw that there was no man, and wondered that there was no intercessor" Isa. 59:16. His delivering mercy depends upon intercessors, who will put their shoulders under the burdens of others. "And I sought for a man among them, that should make up the fence, and stand in the gap before Me for the land, that I should not destroy it: but I found none" Ezek. 22:30. The normal function of prayer is to make intercession with God for others.

### The Mystery of Intercession

That we may pray for others is the deepest mystery and the crowning glory of prayer. If we do not know how to pray for ourselves as we ought, how

can we know how to pray for other people? If we
know so imperfectly our own needs, how can we
know the needs of others? Who are we that we
should presume to interpret the needs of another
to God? He alone knows, and may not His knowledge and love be trusted? The answer is that prayer
cannot be solitary. It must be personal, but it cannot be isolated. Life is relative and interdependent,
"For none of us liveth unto himself" Rom. 14:7.

Prayer cannot stop at personal need. Even in the
inner chamber there is no escape from the impact
of those who impinge upon us in the home, the
church, and the world. The law of prayer is that
each stands alone in the Presence of God, just as
surely as "each one of us shall give account of
himself to God," Rom. 14:12 each bearing his own
burden, and yet every man bearing the burden of
others. There is always a burden. Intercession is
vicarious. The Saviour made intercession because
He bare the sin of the transgressors Isa. 58:12. So
it is in all prayer that entreats for others. Moses
made the cause of Israel his own. (See the prayers
in Exod. 17, 22, 33, 34; Num. 11, 14, 21, 27.)
Isaiah identified himself with the people of "un-
clean lips" Isa. 6:5. Daniel made confession for the
nation Dan. 9. The despairing father of the epilep-
tic boy Mark 9:22 and the distracted mother of the
devil-possessed daughter Matt. 15:21-28 each made
the affliction of the child a personal plea. So it has
been in the history of the Christian Church. Carey
bore the burden of India, Hudson Taylor of China,
Livingstone of Africa; and so does everyone bear
the burden of those for whom he prays.

### The Intercession in Heaven
Prayer is central in Heaven. The interpretation of

the mystery of intercession begins there. It is fellowship in the ministry of our Great High Priest at the right hand of God. "He ever liveth to make intercession" Heb. 7:25. That our Lord should need to pray in the days of His flesh is a mystery of humiliation; that He should need to make intercession in Heaven is a mystery of glory. It is a light that transcends our vision. The "why" and the "how" are beyond our understanding, but it is because He so lives to make intercession that He is able to save to the uttermost all who come to God by Him. The truth revealed is explicit, and its effect in experience assures its certainty. The ascended Christ is the Priest-King at the right hand of God. As High Priest He represents man to God; as King He represents God to man. He entered in by the one offering of Himself as a sacrifice for sin. Having entered by His own blood, He is the One Mediator between God and man, and humanity's Advocate with the Father. He intercedes for men Heb. 7:25, 27; 9:24. Prayer finds its expression and availableness in terms of Christ and His finished work. He takes the prayers of the earthly altar and adds to them the fires of the heavenly, and they become acceptable and effective through His name Heb. 13:15; Rev. 5:8; 8:3. So much is revealed, but it makes clear that in the fellowship of the saints there is prayer in Heaven, and there is no logic by which the redeemed can be excluded from the ministry of intercession.

### The Intercession of the Spirit

There is a two-fold intercession. The High Priest intercedes for us in Heaven, and the Holy Spirit intercedes within the Temple of the consecrated soul. There is such unity of purpose and harmony

of method in the two intercessions that the two are
one, and what is prayed by the Intercessor on earth
is prayed by the Intercessor in Heaven. The Spirit
takes of the things of Christ and reveals them unto
us. He takes of the deep things of God and interprets them to us. He knows the purpose of God,
and makes intercession according to the Divine
will. In this way He works in us both to will and to
do the good pleasure of His will.

Intercession through the Spirit implies a Spirit-
filled Temple. He can only interpret spiritual things
to the spiritually minded, for the carnal mind cannot know the mind of the Spirit. He cannot inter-
cede in the heart of an unyielded will. The pure in
heart see God. The heart must be sensitive to light
and obedient to the heavenly vision. It takes a saint
to be in the ministry of intercession. There are
many kinds of service that make no demand upon
spirituality for their success. Preaching may be an
art in which there is no power of the Spirit. The
ecclesiastical ministry of outer court stewardship
may be rendered by the gifts of the office and the
counter. Social service may make a fair show in
official returns without any glow of spiritual mind-
edness. Church music may be of a kind that does
not call for the travail and anguish of intercession.
The man of prayer must be a man of God.

### The Intercession of the Secret Place

We are called unto the fellowship of this two-fold
intercession. The terms that are used to describe it
indicate sacrificial labor and sustained intensity.
Nothing costs so much. Paul speaks of being in
travail, striving and laboring in prayer. There is always the sweat of blood in prevailing intercession.
The reason is not in God's reluctance, for He in-

spires that He may fulfil. There are many adversaries in the human will, as well as spiritual forces and personalities. God waits to bless; and that means that He is always ready and always waiting. The answer to Daniel's prayer was delayed for three weeks by some mysterious conflict in the realm of spirits Dan. 10:12-14. "For our wrestling," says Paul, "is not against flesh and blood, but against the principalities, against the powers, against the world-rulers of this darkness, against the spiritual hosts of wickedness in the heavenly places" Eph. 6:12. Jesus said, "Satan hath desired to have you, that he may sift you as wheat: but I have prayed for thee" Luke 22:31, 32.

*For whom and for what may we pray?*

The general answer is, for all and for everything. The real answer is, according to the intercession of the Spirit and according to the will of God. There are those who have a natural right to our prayers, such as our families, our friends, our fellow-believers, our minister and colleagues, our fellow-workmen and our employers, as well as those whom we know to be in circumstances of need.

The prayer of intercession calls for intelligence, understanding, watchfulness, as well as for sympathy, intensity, and sacrifice. There is often a severe discipline of patience and faith. Sometimes the answer comes immediately, and sometimes it does not. The one truth in which faith rests is that it comes. The Spirit that assures is acquainted with all contingencies, and His assurances are YEA and AMEN in Christ Jesus.

I have been more mindful to set forth the sanctuary of my own faith than to give rules and to quote examples. The subject is in all the Scriptures, and its range is without boundaries. Its mysteries are unsearchable, but its certainties are infallible. The blessings are immeasurable and invaluable. Who can tell the influences that have come into his life through the intercession of those who have prayed for him?

Who can measure the work of those whose ministry is that of laboring in prayer for others? The great need of God is for intercessors. "Ye that are the Lord's remembrancers, take ye no rest, and give Him no rest, till He establish, and till He make Jerusalem a praise in the earth" Isa. 62:6, 7.

He still saves by them that sigh and that cry.

# 15. The Problem of Unanswered Prayer

It is many years since I first wrote on unanswered prayer. The problem became acute when the man for whom we were praying so earnestly and confidently died while we prayed. We went back to the Word, and God gave me a message that has brought consolation to many, and through all the years it has been a stronghold for my trust. Many years have passed, but the truth abides, and though it may involve some repetition, I want to pass on the message to others.

### The Problem

There can be no doubt that God answers prayer. On this point the Scriptures speak plainly enough. Nothing could be more definite. Assurances that prayer is heard abound. The promises are explicit, and the Scriptures are full of examples and encouragement. Christ's own word is, "Every one that asketh receiveth" Matt. 7:8. The scope of the promise is without limit of place 1 Tim. 2:8, time Luke 18:1; 1 Tim. 4:17, or subject John 16:23; Matt. 21:22; Phil. 4:6. Everything that concerns man is of interest to God, and is a proper subject for prayer. God does not divide our needs into sacred and secular, spiritual and material. He who taught us to pray for the forgiveness of our sins, taught us also to say, "Give us this day our daily bread."

Yet, as we have studied the subject, it has been made clear that there are conditions and limitations. There are laws of prayer. The unrestricted promises are hedged with conditions. We are commanded to pray for all men, but there were some for whom the prophet was forbidden to pray Jer. 7:16, see also 1 John 5: 15, 16. It is possible to ask and not receive Ps. 66:18; James 4:2, 3. Prayers that lack sincerity and faith cannot be heard. This is obvious. God judges by the heart. So do we. No one grants requests where these simple elements are wanting. The sincerity must extend to both petition and petitioner. Eloquence is not prayer Isa. 29:13; John 9:31; James 4:6; John 3:22.

*Are all the sincere, earnest, believing prayers of good people granted?*

The answer of experience is, No. I have seen a distracted mother cling to the corpse of her child, refusing to believe it was dead. She had prayed. God had promised. She had believed. He heard, always heard. How could her child die? When at last the truth has forced itself upon her protesting mind, the distress deepens at the thought that God has not heard. There are many such days of desperate faith. Is God angry as in the case of David, 2 Sam. 12:14-23, even though there be no such cause? Can it be that He is indifferent? Can it be that He does not know? Has He forgotten? Is it any use to pray? It was with such thoughts as these that I turned to my Bible, and found the answer in three representative cases:

1. Deut. 3:23-35, where Moses prayed that he might go over into Canaan.
2. I Kings 29:4. Elijah's prayer that he might die.
3. 2 Cor. 12:8, 9, in which Paul prayed for the removal of affliction.

These three men occupy a prominent place in Scripture, and yet each was denied his request. Their prayers are fairly representative, and cover the ground of the problem.

### The Prayer of Moses

Moses prayed that he might be allowed to complete his work. He had undertaken it at God's command. For forty years he had nursed and led a murmuring and ungrateful people through the wilderness. The promised land was within sight. What more natural than that he should desire to see his life-work completed? Besides, to all human judgment he could not be spared. He would be needed in Canaan even more than in the wilderness. There were enemies to be driven out, the constitution to be established, and the people to be settled. If he should leave them now, the work of forty years would fall to pieces. Internal strife would wreck the nation. No wonder he prayed that he might go over. In spite of a nation's entreaty, regardless of his record, and notwithstanding his earnest pleading, he died; died with his work unfinished; died when he seemed to be most needed; died with the hope of years at last within his reach.

Is it not often so?

A lifework is accepted as a Divine appointment. The powers of brain and muscle, time and energy, all a man is goes into the task at the cost of personal comfort and ambition. You pray for your work, that God will prosper it and bless you in it. That is right. No man has a right to be in any business for which he connot pray. God does not put a man into business for worthless or unworthy ends. He means the work to prosper; and yet how often it happens that the prayers of good men seem to fail. Plans over which they have prayed collapse. Competitors prevail. Misfortune overwhelms. Ill health disables. Death calls, and the work of years is left unfinished. Death at such times seems almost spiteful in its cruelty. It strikes the arm as it stretches the hand to grasp the prize; takes the parent and counsellor when he can least be spared; passes by the weak and takes the strong; strikes down the burden-bearer and spares the burden. We plead that we may stay a little longer: only a little while; just till this is completed; just till the children are grown up, or the business settled; the answer is, "Get thee up into the top of Pisgah"—and die. David wanted to build a House for God. His heart was set on it. God praised him for wanting to do it, but He forbade him 1 Chron. 22:8. So is many a heart set with a yearning that prays and aches for a work that is withheld. The man Jesus saved with a mighty salvation prayed that he might go with Jesus, and Jesus sent him home Luke 8:38.

God answered all Elijah's prayers but one, and that was the prayer that he might die. He was under the juniper tree, suffering from mental and physical reaction. Yesterday had been a great day. He had stood alone as God's champion: strong, defiant, triumphant. The next day was the day after! At the threat of a woman he fled. His nerves were unstrung. Fear, despondency, and despair took hold of him. In depression he prayed that he might die. The disease is still with us, and is so multiplied that there are not enough juniper trees to go round. There are morbid Christians who have built tabernacles under them. Nerve collapse is more spiritual than physical, though it is usually both. There is no despondency in faith. What a mercy God does not always take us at our word. Nothing dishonors God more than the fretful despondency of the saints. Juniper trees make poor sanctuaries.

The Apostle's thorn in the flesh need not detain us, for we have already dealt with the subject of prayer and affliction. The thorn was a physical affliction, and because he regarded it as a hindrance he prayed for its removal. It was not removed, though he besought the Lord three times. He had to learn that affliction may be God's messenger, as well as the messenger of Satan.

### The Answer to Unanswered Prayers

None of these prayers was unanswered. They were not granted, but they were answered, and "No" was the answer. "No" is as truly an answer as "Yes." When a request is refused, it is as truly answered as when it is granted. Refusal may be the only answer possible to love and wisdom and truth.

A child may cry for a razor, and full-grown people may cry for things equally unsuitable, unsafe, and unwise. Many have lived to thank God that He withstood their agonizing entreaties at some particular time or for some particular thing that seemed indispensable.

God never refuses without reason. He knows the past, in which there may be reasons for present disqualification. Forgiven sin may disable. Moses and David were both examples of this Deut. 32:49-52; 2 Sam. 12:14. There are vessels that break on the wheel, and though another may be made, the original is impossible. Diseases may be healed, but a lost limb cannot be restored. The Lord knows the future as well as the past. The immediate may imperil the future. The eagerness for a mess of pottage may involve the loss of an inheritance. Esau got the answer to his entreaty at dinnertime. Jacob got his at dawn. God spared Hezekiah fifteen years, but he had better have gone when the Lord sent for him.

#### The Greater Includes the Less

Delays are not denials, and it pays to wait God's time. Moses got into Canaan, and Elijah went to heaven by a more glorious way than that of the juniper tree. No inspired prayer of faith is ever refused. "No" is never God's last word. If the prayer seems unanswered, it is because it is lost in the glory of the answer when it comes. God may refuse the route because He knows a better way. He took Moses into Canaan by a better way and in better company. I have known other people who have had to go by way of heaven to find the answer to their prayers. He took Elijah to heaven by a much more wonderful way than that of the grave. Elijah wanted to die, and God gave His tired servant sleep and rest, and sent him away to the hills for a holiday. That is His remedy for nerves: a change of air, a new vision, and a bigger job. Paul never had any use for juniper trees, and to him God said, "My grace is sufficient for thee," and He taught him to glory in affliction and adversity. In the experience that first sorely tried our faith, God sent help out of the darkness. Through the tears of a broken heart the vision came, and when the memorial card was sent it bore this text, which rebuked our unbelief, "He asked life of Thee, and Thou gavest it him, even length of days for ever and ever" Ps. 21:4. So in Glory shall we find our prayers have been interpreted according to the infinite wisdom and eternal love of God our Father, Who bids us pray

*"Unanswered yet! The prayers your lips have pleaded*
   *In agony of heart these many years?*
*Does faith begin to fail? Is hope departing?*
   *And think you all in vain those falling tears?*
*Say not, the Father hath not heard your prayer,*
   *You shall have your desire–sometime–somewhere.*

*"Unanswered yet! Though when you first presented*
   *This one petition at the Father's Throne*
*It seemed you could not wait the time of asking,*
   *So urgent was the heart to make it known;*
*Though years have passed since then, do not despair,*
   *The Lord will answer you–sometime–somewhere.*

*"Unanswered yet! Nay, do not say ungranted,*
   *Perhaps your work is not wholly done.*
*The work began when first your prayer was uttered,*
   *And God will finish what He has begun.*
*If you will keep the incense burning there,*
   *His glory you shall see–sometime–somewhere.*

"Unanswered yet! Faith cannot be unanswered;
　　Her feet are firmly planted on the Rock;
　Amid the wildest storms she stands undaunted,
　　Nor quails before the loudest thunder shock.
　She knows Omnipotence has heard her prayer,
　　And cries, 'It shall be done—sometime—somewhere.'"

*E. B. Browning.*